I0820094

The
Hoosier Mama
BOOK OF
BREAKFAST
BAKES

The Hoosier Mama BOOK OF BREAKFAST BAKES

BISCUITS, SCONES, MUFFINS, *and More*

PAULA HANEY

A MIDWAY BOOK

AGATE

CHICAGO

First printed in December 2025

Printed in China

10 9 8 7 6 5 4 3 2 1 25 26 27 28 29

ISBN-13: 978-1-57284-359-2 (hardcover)
ISBN-10: 1-5728435-9-4 (hardcover)
eISBN-13: 978-1-57284-903-7 (ebook)
eISBN-10: 1-57284-903-7 (ebook)

Art direction and cover design by Morgan Krehbiel
Photography by Laura Scherb
Food styling on pages 21, 31, 36, 57, 69, and 109 by Jessica Ellington

Cataloging in Publication data is available from the Library of Congress

Midway Books is an imprint of Agate Publishing. Agate books are available in bulk at discount prices. For more information, visit agatepublishing.com.

FOR CRAIG, DASHIELL, AND ESME,
MY FAVORITE BREAKFAST COMPANIONS.

CONTENTS

Hoosier Mama
PIE COMPANY

INTRODUCTION

When we opened our first Hoosier Mama Pie Shop fifteen years ago in Chicago's Ukrainian Village neighborhood, our goal, to many people's astonishment, was to open a bakery that made just one thing—pie. With one employee, two ovens, and a grand total of 750 square feet, we didn't have much choice. All of our space—physical, emotional, and mental—was taken up by pie 24/7. After a few weeks, we added some scones so folks who stopped in to pick up a pie on their way to work would have something to eat with their coffee. We chose scones because they bake at a high temperature and could easily fit in the ovens among the fruit pies we baked every morning. Next, we added berry-packed muffins for the farmers' market, to take advantage of the summer fruit that was coming in and out of season faster than we could come up with new pie recipes.

When we opened our Evanston location, we suddenly had more space, more customers, and several feet of display cases to fill. Plus, we opened at an alarming 6:30 a.m. and, as it turns out, not everyone wants pie for breakfast. Did we sit down and plot out a pastry program based on market research and current trends? We did not. We made the things we wanted to eat, from the jam-stuffed cornbread muffins to the brioche Danishes with passion fruit curd and fresh blackberries. As always, we baked seasonally and took inspiration from local ingredients.

The good news is, unlike pie, most of the recipes in this book go from idea to eating in under an hour. We hope this is a book kept on the kitchen counter, ready at a moment's notice when you bring home the first rhubarb of the season from the farmers' market or discover a forgotten pint of strawberries in the back of the fridge. We hope its pages get stuck together with maple syrup and a dusting of flour falls out every time you open it. Consider this a working manual and don't be afraid to write your own variations and additions in the margins.

HOW TO USE THIS BOOK

While some folks are most comfortable working with traditional measuring cups and spoons, others wouldn't think of following a recipe that wasn't written out in grams. We've written all of the recipes in this book both ways: Gram measurements appear in the right-hand column of the ingredients lists, while all other measurements are on the left. Simply choose the version you like best and read the ingredients from top to bottom. Occasionally, an ingredient, like nutmeg, is too light to weigh. If no weight is listed in the gram column, use the volume measurement for the ingredient instead.

Whichever version you choose, be sure to read the recipe at least once before you start. No one wants to discover halfway through that they are missing a crucial ingredient or don't have the right size pan. Following the steps in order is important, either for efficiency, success of the final product, or both.

Fancy, expensive equipment can be fun, but it is certainly not necessary. The most important thing is to get to know your oven. I once worked in a fine-dining restaurant where the oven sloped so much that we had to shove a spoon under the sheet pans to bake level crème brûlées.

Oven temperatures vary more than you'd think. Consider buying an oven thermometer, which costs a few dollars at the grocery store and could save you some headaches. This book's baking times and temperatures are for standard conventional ovens found in most home kitchens. If you have a convection oven option, decrease the oven temperatures by 50 degrees and the baking time by about 20 percent.

Please keep in mind that all baking times are estimates. Ovens vary widely, and all sorts of things, from weather to the temperature of ingredients, can affect baking times. All the recipes include tests besides time to determine if a pastry is done. When in doubt, follow your nose! Most baked goods are the most aromatic right before they are done.

SEASONALITY

At Hoosier Mama, we bake with the seasons. We make blueberry muffins when we can get blueberries straight from local farmers and ramp biscuits when the ramps peek out of the warming ground. We like being part of the seasons, and we're lucky to have a farm community around us that makes that easy. I, too, enjoy the convenience of grabbing a pint of strawberries at the grocery store any time of year, but the flavor can't match a local berry in June. Some of my favorite foods, like ramps, American persimmons, and black raspberries, can be found only at farmers' markets since they don't play well with large-scale commercial shipping.

As a local bakery, our job is to showcase local foodways, but it is also our job to make delicious pastries, and baking with local fruit in season is an easy way to up your baking game. A peach picked ripe from the tree is going to be delicious in a muffin or pie without much help from me, and while we are sad when that peach goes out of season, we know that perfectly ripe pears are just around the corner. Don't be afraid to swap out the fruit in your favorite recipes as the seasons change.

TOOLS

You don't need a lot of fancy equipment to make the recipes in this book. For recipes that call for very specific pans or molds, we've tried to suggest other options that you probably already own or that will serve more than one purpose if you have to purchase them. That said, always buy the best equipment you can reasonably afford. You deserve quality tools. A surprising amount of bad home cooking is just due to bad equipment. Muffins, scones, and biscuits burn in flimsy grocery store pans, and no amount of skill in the kitchen will change that. Look for equipment that is easy to clean and durable. Don't forget to include a few tools that make you happy. I have an acacia wood spoon that's the perfect size and weight for my hand. It is beautiful. It makes me happy. I use it for every meal I cook. That's a lot of happiness.

RIMMED BAKING SHEETS (ALSO CALLED HALF AND QUARTER SHEET PANS)

Baking sheets are the workhorses of the kitchen. Made of heavy-gauge aluminum, they heat up and cool down quickly and maintain an even heat across the surface for consistent baking and roasting. A half sheet measures 18 × 13 inches, which is perfect for most ovens. Quarter sheets measure 9½ × 13 inches and fit two to an oven rack so you can bake several items at once. Both sizes have a 1-inch rim, so they double as brownie, cornbread, or sheet cake pans. I use them for baking cookies, pastries, scones, and biscuits, for roasting vegetables, and for making sheet-pan dinners. They come in nonstick options, but I like the durability of the uncoated sheets; simply spray them with cooking spray or line them with parchment paper. All aluminum pans discolor in the dishwasher, but the damage is purely aesthetic. Confusingly, the lower the gauge, the heavier the material; 14 to 18 gauge is a good-quality option without breaking the bank.

MUFFIN TINS (ALSO CALLED CUPCAKE PANS)

Muffin tins come in a variety of materials. Look for pans made from heavy-gauge aluminized steel for best results. Avoid silicone pans, cute as they are, for anything other than the tiniest of muffins. These pans don't conduct heat well and lead to underbrowning the bottoms and sides of muffins. They also become flimsy and hard to handle when hot. Choose pans with a nonstick coating if you want to skip muffin liners. Chicago Metallic, OXO, and USA Pan are some reliable options.

PORTION SCOOPS (ALSO CALLED DISHERS)

Portion scoops come in a range of sizes from less than a tablespoon to 1 cup. They are identified by the color of the handle and a corresponding number. They are handy for scooping muffins, quick breads, cookies, ice cream, and much more. Find them on Amazon or Webstaurant, an online restaurant supply store. The sidebar shows the sizes we use again and again.

#6	white	⅔ cup
#8	gray	½ cup
#12	green	⅓ cup
#16	blue	¼ cup
#20	yellow	3 tablespoons plus 1 teaspoon
#40	orchid	1 tablespoon plus 1 teaspoon

PASTRY BRUSHES

This is an essential tool for evenly applying everything from egg wash to barbecue sauce. Old-school brushes with boar bristles soak up liquid and work best for thin washes like butter, eggs, oil, or cream. Look for lacquered hardwood handles and plastic collars where the bristles attach to the handle. Silicone brushes with thin silicone bristles work best for heavy or sticky sauces like honey or maple syrup.

BENCH KNIFE

A bench knife is a baker's favorite tool! It has a rectangular, stainless steel blade with a handle on one side. The blade is just sharp enough to portion dough, cube butter, and roughly chop nuts. The wide, flat blade is great for scooping up chopped herbs or other ingredients. Handles can be plastic, rolled metal, or wood. Take the time to try out several options—you'll be using this a lot. OXO makes a nice one with a squishy silicone handle that keeps your hand from getting tired.

INSTANT-READ THERMOMETER

A reliable instant-read thermometer takes the guesswork out of cooking and baking, particularly if you are making a recipe for the first time. It's also essential for food safety when heating and cooling foods. Go ahead and spring for a waterproof model that is dishwasher safe. It's the one thing I always pack when I travel if I'm staying somewhere with a kitchen.

OVEN THERMOMETER

Oven thermometers are cheap and essential. It's not unusual for even new, high-end ovens to be off by 25 to 50 degrees or more.

HANDHELD CITRUS JUICER

Simple, inexpensive, and efficient, citrus juicers come in three different sizes for oranges, lemons, and limes. Choose the stainless steel or brightly colored enameled versions; avoid uncoated aluminum models that can react with acidic citrus juice.

BISCUIT CUTTERS

If you make biscuits regularly, you'll need at least one good sturdy cutter. Biscuit cutters are much stronger than cookie cutters since they must slice through dense, sticky dough without warping. They must also be thin enough to cut cleanly so the biscuits rise evenly. Look for stainless steel cutters with securely riveted handles. We keep several Hulisen 2¾-inch square cutters with soft-grip handles on hand for biscuits and scones, but they come in all shapes and sizes. A set of graduated cutters is nice so you have lots of options.

MICROPLANE ZESTER

Invented in the '90s as a fine wood rasp, the Microplane zester was strictly a woodworking tool until the wife of a Canadian hardware store owner grabbed it one day to add orange zest to cake batter. Its row of tiny teeth shaves the peel from citrus fruit, leaving the bitter pith behind. Use it to finely grate nutmeg and chocolate too. Today there are dozens of different versions and sizes from many manufacturers, but my favorite is still the Microplane Classic Zester. Available at kitchen supply stores, the gadget aisle of upscale grocery stores, and at Microplane.com.

ROLLING PINS

The best rolling pin is the one that works for you. At the shop, we like dowel-style baker's pins with no handles. They take some getting used to since you guide the pin with your palms rather than by gripping handles. We think it makes it easier to put consistent pressure on the dough, and positioning your hands closer to the dough makes rolling more intuitive. The sleek design is easy to clean. Antiques of Tomorrow (Antiques-of-Tomorrow.square.site), Fletchers' Mill (FletchersMill.com), and JK Adams (JKAdams.com) all craft multiple styles of pins from beautiful hardwoods.

DIGITAL SCALE

We love that kitchen scales have become easier to find (I picked up my last one on a grocery run) and less expensive to buy since we wrote the last book. Ozeri makes a reliable model for under twenty bucks. Escali, Taylor, and OXO are also good brands to try. Look for a scale with at least a 10-pound capacity and 1-gram weight increments.

PARCHMENT PAPER

Baker's parchment paper keeps biscuits, scones, and cookies from sticking and makes cleanup easy. If you have the space, ordering a big box of precut half-sheet-pan-sized parchment sheets online is economical and convenient. It also comes in rolls that are easy to find in upscale grocery stores and specialty cooking stores.

TOMATO CORER

I've never used one of these to core a tomato—a paring knife works just fine—but I do use it to remove the core and stem from peeled apples and pears before I chop them and to hull strawberries. I find that the inexpensive ones work best.

TIMERS

Shout-out to the IKEA Fantast Digital Meat Thermometer/Timer, the only timer we've found that's tough enough to stand up to a commercial kitchen. It has strong magnets for attaching to a cooler and a sturdy metal foot for setting on the counter. It's encircled in a thick soft-grip bumper so it survives falls. A metal face and silicone buttons make it easy to clean and water resistant. Switch it to thermometer mode with a detachable corded metal probe. You can even set the alarm to sound when food reaches a preset temperature, which is handy for making candies and syrups. IKEA doesn't sell them online, so you'll have to go to a store to pick them up—along with some Swedish fish and meatballs.

VEGETABLE PEELER

The Kuhn Rikon Original Swiss Peeler is the best investment you can make for your kitchen—for under ten dollars. These peelers are durable, effective, and comfortable to use.

LOAF PANS

The best loaf pans are made from aluminized steel. They are sturdy, conduct heat well, and produce a nicely browned loaf without burning the bottom. However, I'm also a sucker for cute glass, Pyrex, and ceramic versions, especially the vintage ones, and I am not going to tell you not to use them. Keep in mind that glass and ceramic take longer to heat up and may need extra baking time.

INGREDIENTS

SOURCING INGREDIENTS

Chocolate

You can find any chocolate you need on Amazon. We especially like Callebaut, Cacao Barry, Guittard, Scharffen Berger, or Valrhona.

- Callebaut.com
- Cacao-barry.com
- Guittard.com
- ScharffenBerger.com
- Valrhona.com

Coarse-Grained Sugar (Disco Sugar)

We use large (size AA) decorative sugar crystals, available at Amazon or Bake Deco.

- BakeDeco.com

Country Ham

We use traditional country ham to make our Red-Eye Gravy (page 152) and to top our biscuits. Unless you live in the South, mail order is probably your only option. We tried Browning's Country Ham, Dan'l Boone Inn Country Ham, and Col. Bill Newsom's Aged Kentucky Country Ham. Find more options on the National Country Ham Association website under the "Where to Buy" tab.

- BrowningsCountryHam.com
- NewsomsCountryHam.com
- CountryHam.org

Farmers' Markets and Resources for Local, Sustainable Food

We are lucky to be a vendor at the Green City Market in Chicago, where we often pick up seasonal produce from Ellis Family Farms, Klüg Farms, Nichols Farm and Orchard, and Seedling Farms. To find a farmers' market in your area, go to the National Farmers' Market Directory and enter your town or zip code.

- NFMD.org
- EllisFamilyFarms.com
- MickKlugFarms.com
- NicholsFarm.com
- GreenCityMarket.org

Flour and Cornmeal

Ceresota (sold as Heckers on the East Coast) is "unbleached forever," as the sack says. This is a good all-purpose flour that's been around forever. King Arthur Baking is another good source for specialty flours as well as baking ingredients and equipment. Their all-purpose flour is available in most grocery stores across the country. Brian Severson Farms/Quality Organic is an organic, non-GMO grain farm in Illinois that stone-grinds its flour and cornmeal. They're our source for heirloom red, blue, and yellow cornmeal, oats, buckwheat, and whole wheat pastry flour.

- HeckersCeresota.com
- KingArthurBaking.com
- QualityOrganic.com

Fruit Purees

We use Ravifruit passion fruit puree to make our passion fruit curd. Look for it online at Gourmet Food Store, iGourmet, and Amazon. It's a bit pricey and it seems to go in and out of stock frequently. If you need to substitute a different brand, choose a puree with 10 percent sugar, like La Fruitiere.

- GourmetFoodStore.com
- iGourmet.com
- Amazon.com

Gelatin Sheets, Silver Strength

We use silver strength gelatin sheets to add body and structure to our curds and pastry cream. They are available online at Modernist Pantry or Amazon. Any brand is fine.

- ModernistPantry.com

Maple Syrup

We recommend pure maple syrup for our Maple-Bacon (page 97) and Maple-Pecan Scones (page 84) and to pour over Biscuit French Toast Casserole (page 160). For the best maple flavor, look for syrup labeled Dark, Extra Dark, Robust, or Strong (formerly labeled Grade B). Burton's Maplewood Farm, Spring Hill Farm, and Morley's Maple Syrup are good online options. If you live on the East Coast or in the Midwest, check your favorite farmers' market for a local sugarmaker.

- BurtonsMaplewoodFarm.com
- MorleysMapleSyrup.com
- SpringHillFarmVT.com

Meat

In Chicago, we get sustainable turkey, chicken, pork, lamb, beef, and sausage directly from the farmers at Slagel Farms, Mint Creek Farm, Finn's Ranch, and Jake's Country Meats. Visit your local farmers' market to find a farmer in your area.

- SlagelFarms.com
- MintCreekFarm.com
- FinnsRanch.com
- JakesCountryMeats.com

Mushrooms

River Valley Ranch and Kitchens sells mushrooms grown on their Wisconsin farm and small-batch mushroom products like salsa, pasta sauce, mushroom burgers, and more at their farm shop in Burlington, Wisconsin, at farmers' markets in Wisconsin and Illinois, including Chicago's Green City Market, and online.

- RvrValley.com

Persimmon Pulp

To make our Persimmon Muffins (page 57), you'll need persimmon pulp. I like to drive rural southern Indiana lanes in the fall until I find a hand-lettered sign for a farmer selling frozen pulp. You can also buy it online from Fischer Farms or Integration Acres.

- FFNatural.com
- IntegrationAcres.com

Signs of fall in Parke County, Indiana

Sorghum Syrup

To make our Red-Eye Gravy (page 152) and Sorghum and Butter (page 149), you'll need sorghum syrup (also called sorghum molasses or just sorghum), available from Col. Bill Newsom's Aged Kentucky Country Ham or the Loveless Café.

- NewsomsCountryHam.com
- LovelessCafe.com

Spices

We recommend Penzeys for spices; you can order online or use the store locator to find a shop near you. Another great online option is Burlap and Barrel.

- Penzeys.com
- BurlapAndBarrel.com

Urban Honey

To find a honey producer near you, visit the National Honey Board website and click the locator tab. We get ours from Sweet Beginnings, the Chicago Honey Co-op, and Bike a Bee.

- Honey.com
- BeeLoveBuzz.com/Sweet-Beginnings
- ChicagoHoneyCoop.com
- BikeaBee.com

Vanilla Bean Paste

We use Nielsen-Massey.

- NielsenMassey.com

MEASURING SALT

Professional bakers love kosher salt. It brings out the flavors in food without overwhelming them or turning bitter like iodized table salt.

Measuring kosher salt, however, can be tricky. While table salt is finely ground and packs together tightly, kosher salt comes in big irregular flakes that leave lots of empty space in between. So, a teaspoon of table salt contains up to twice as much salt as a teaspoon of kosher salt. To make matters worse, different brands of kosher salt have different flake sizes and shapes, making it impossible to swap brands one for one.

We use Diamond Crystal kosher salt, for no other reason than it was stocked in my first professional kitchen. All the volume measurements in this book are accurate for that brand only. Your best bet is to measure salt by weight. All salt is interchangeable by weight, so 6 grams of one type of salt is equal to 6 grams of any other type of salt. As always, when in doubt, don't forget to taste!

Here is a rough guideline:

1 teaspoon Diamond Crystal kosher salt

= ⅝ teaspoon Morton's kosher salt

= ½ teaspoon table salt

CHAPTER 1

Muffins

Let's be honest. Muffins are an excuse to eat cake for breakfast; no one is mad about that. Muffins are a great place to start if you are new to baking and a great place to land if you want something satisfying and seasonal in the shortest amount of time. Despite their ease to make, pulling a warm pan of muffins out of the oven for breakfast is always impressive. A friend once surprised his girlfriend with freshly baked muffins for her birthday, only to have her insist he must have snuck out and bought them, convinced that "you need special equipment to make muffins." Aside from a muffin tin, this is not true.

Muffins are best mixed by hand and only until the ingredients are barely combined. It's crucial not to overmix. Any additions, like chocolate chips or blueberries, should be added while there are still streaks of flour in the batter. The batter may be lumpy. That's OK. Muffins should bake up with rounded tops and an even, delicate crumb. Overmixing the batter overdevelops the gluten in the flour and keeps the muffins from rising. The resulting muffins are dense, flat, and full of air pockets. The most frequent mistake bakers in our kitchen (including myself) have made over the years is overmixing muffin batter.

HOW TO FOLD

After adding the wet ingredients to the flour mixture (facing page, top left), bring the spatula down through the center of the bowl. Turn the spatula over (top right). Give the bowl a quarter turn and repeat the process of bringing the spatula through the center of the bowl and turning it over until just a few streaks of flour remain (bottom left). Finally, add any mix-ins and finish it off with a couple of quick folds (bottom right).

Top left: Pouring mixed wet ingredients into the dry ingredients
Top right: Gently folding the wet and dry ingredients together
Bottom left: Continuing to fold until a few streaks of flour remain
Bottom right: Adding mix-ins and folding until all flour is incorporated

MUFFIN TINS

Muffin pans or tins come in three basic sizes: mini, standard, and jumbo. Interestingly, there is little consensus on what these terms actually mean. Standard pans are the most common, usually measuring 2¾ × 2 × 1½ inches (the top diameter, bottom diameter, and depth of each muffin compartment) and holding ½ cup if filled to the rim, although there may be slight variations among manufacturers.

Jumbo pans are anything bigger than a standard pan. Jumbo pans may hold 6, 7, 8, or more ounces, and dimensions vary quite a bit across brands. Mini pans usually hold just 1 to 2 ounces. At the shop, we use an 8-ounce jumbo pan with compartments measuring 3¾ × 2½ × 2 inches. For the purposes of this book, this is the definition of a jumbo pan. Most of the recipes in this book will make 12 standard or 6 jumbo muffins (as defined by me!). Unless a recipe states otherwise, fill standard muffin cups with ⅓ cup of batter. Fill jumbo muffin cups with ⅔ cup of batter. If you are going to bake a lot of muffins, consider investing in some dishers or portion scoops. We use them for muffins, cookies, and all kinds of projects in the kitchen. A green (#12) scoop works great for standard muffins. A white (#6) scoop is perfect for jumbo muffins. If you have a different-size pan or want to make mini muffins (they are adorable), fill the muffin cavities three-quarters full.

At the shop, we line our muffin tins with paper muffin cups. They make the muffins easy to remove from the pans and keep them fresher longer. They also make cleanup a breeze. You can also grease the muffin tins with butter or coat them with cooking spray. Buttering the muffin tins makes the bottom of the muffins taste slightly fried, which I really like. If your muffins are still sticking to the pan, try dusting the greased pans with flour.

Butter-Based Muffin Base

This is our go-to muffin recipe. It started as a classic blueberry muffin but handled every variation we threw at it so deliciously we kept adding more. We've included a chart of the variations we've come up with so far (see page 24). Don't hesitate to add your own. Because different variations call for different amounts of extra ingredients, some flavors make a little extra batter. We solve that problem in the shop by baking the extra batter in a small pie tin or loaf pan and slicing it up for kitchen snacks. Most muffin batters can be held for up to 2 days in the refrigerator before baking. Muffin batters with strawberries and raspberries hold for only 1 day in the refrigerator before the berries get too juicy.

Ingredients

Yield: 12 standard muffins or 6 jumbo muffins

¾ cup	**whole milk**	170g
½ cup (1 stick)	**unsalted butter**	113g
2 ⅓ cups	**all-purpose flour**	280g
¾ cup	**granulated sugar**	150g
¼ cup	**packed dark brown sugar**	53g
1 tablespoon	**baking powder**	12g
¾ teaspoon	**kosher salt**	2.25g
2	**large eggs**	100g
1 teaspoon	**vanilla paste**	5g
	Optional spices, additions, and/or toppings (see page 24)	

1 Preheat the oven to 375°F. Prepare a muffin tin with paper liners.

2 Combine the milk and butter in a small saucepan. Heat over medium heat, stirring occasionally, until the butter is almost melted. Remove from the heat and let cool until the butter is completely melted and the mixture is lukewarm.

3 In a large bowl, whisk together the flour, granulated sugar, brown sugar, baking powder, salt, and any additional spices.

4 Crack the eggs into a medium bowl. Add the vanilla and whisk to break up the yolks. Slowly whisk the milk mixture into the eggs.

5 Add the wet ingredients to the flour mixture and fold with a wooden spoon or silicone spatula until just a few streaks of flour remain. Gently fold in any additions.

6 For jumbo muffins, scoop ½ cup batter into each muffin cup. For standard muffins, scoop ¼ to ⅓ cup batter into each muffin cup. Top the muffins with any optional toppings.

7 Bake standard muffins for 20 to 25 minutes and jumbo muffins for 25 to 30 minutes, until they are firm to the touch and a toothpick inserted in the middle comes out clean.

Most muffin batters can be stored for up to 2 days in the refrigerator before baking, but muffin batters with strawberries and raspberries will hold for only 1 day in the refrigerator before the berries get too juicy. Muffins are best enjoyed the same day but can be stored overnight in an airtight container at room temperature. Revive tired muffins by splitting, toasting, and spreading with butter.

PREP NOTE Do not overmix the batter!

BUTTER-BASED MUFFIN VARIATIONS

These are some of our favorite ways to use the Butter-Based Muffin Base recipe on page 22. Don't hesitate to add your own!

Variation	Additional Ingredients	Suggested Toppings
Cranberry-Walnut	• 1 cup chopped cranberries • 1 cup chopped walnuts • Grated zest of 1 orange • ½ teaspoon ground ginger	• Walnut Crumble (page 294) • Sanding sugar
Cranberry-Ginger	• 1 cup chopped cranberries • Grated zest of 1 orange • ½ teaspoon ground ginger	• Sanding sugar (if you want extra oomph, rub the sugar with orange zest and a little ground ginger) • Chopped candied ginger
Orange–Chocolate Chip (full recipe page 32)	• Grated zest of 1 orange • 1 cup chocolate chips	• Sanding sugar
Mixed Berry	• Grated zest of 1 lemon • 2 cups mixed berries	• Walnut Crumble (page 294) • Oat Crumble (page 295) • Cinnamon Streusel (page 276) • Lemon Glaze (page 291) • Sherry Vinegar Icing (page 290) • Sanding sugar
Blueberry (full recipe page 27)	• Grated zest of 1 lemon • 2 cups blueberries	• Walnut Crumble (page 294) • Oat Crumble (page 295) • Cinnamon Streusel (page 276) • Lemon Glaze (page 291) • Sherry Vinegar Icing (page 290) • Sanding sugar
Grape-Walnut (full recipe page 30)	• 1½ cups halved grapes • 1 cup walnuts, roughly chopped	• Roughly chopped walnuts • Walnut Crumble (page 294) • Sanding sugar
Pear-Cardamom	• 1 cup chopped pear • 1½ teaspoons vanilla paste (replaces 1 teaspoon in base recipe) • ½ teaspoon ground cardamom	• Orange Glaze (page 291)

Variation	Additional Ingredients	Suggested Toppings
Rhubarb	• 2 cups peeled and chopped rhubarb, cut into roughly 1-inch pieces	• Walnut or Pecan Crumble (page 294) • Oat Crumble (page 295) • Cinnamon Streusel (page 276) • Lemon Glaze (page 291) • Sherry Vinegar Icing (page 290) • Sanding sugar • Granulated sugar
Strawberry-Rhubarb	• ½ cup halved (or quartered if large) strawberries • ¾ cup peeled and chopped rhubarb, cut into 1- to 2-inch pieces	• Walnut Crumble (page 294) • Oat Crumble (page 295) • Cinnamon Streusel (page 276) • Lemon Glaze (page 291) • Sherry Vinegar Icing (page 290) • Sanding sugar
Apple	• 2 cups peeled and chopped apples • ½ teaspoon Chinese five-spice powder	• Walnut or Pecan Crumble (page 294) • Oat Crumble (page 295) • Cinnamon Streusel (page 276) • Sanding sugar
Raspberry	• 2 cups raspberries • Grated zest of 1 orange	• Walnut or Pecan Crumble (page 294) • Oat Crumble (page 295) • Cinnamon Streusel (page 276) • Lemon Glaze (page 291) • Sherry Vinegar Icing (page 290) • Sanding sugar
Strawberry (full recipe page 34)	• 2 cups halved (or quartered if large) strawberries	• Walnut Crumble (page 294) • Oat Crumble (page 295) • Cinnamon Streusel (page 276) • Lemon Glaze (page 291) • Orange Glaze (page 291) • Sherry Vinegar Icing (page 290) • Sanding sugar

Gently fold any additional ingredients in at the end of Step 5 (page 23), and add any suggested toppings at the end of Step 6. Remember not to overmix the batter!

Blueberry Muffins

Blueberry is the most popular muffin flavor in the United States. In fact, it is so beloved in Minnesota they made it the state . . . muffin? Minnesotan or not, we all celebrate National Blueberry Muffin Day on July 11. At Hoosier Mama, we pack as many fresh blueberries into our blueberry muffins as possible. Our customers love them, and so do we. We bake them nearly every day when the berries are in season, from June to early fall.

Ingredients

Yield: 12 standard muffins or 6 jumbo muffins

¾ cup	**whole milk**	170g
½ cup (1 stick)	**unsalted butter**	113g
2⅓ cups	**all-purpose flour**	280g
¾ cup	**granulated sugar**	150g
¼ cup	**packed dark brown sugar**	53g
1 tablespoon	**baking powder**	12g
¾ teaspoon	**kosher salt**	2.25g
	Grated zest of 1 lemon	
2	**large eggs**	100g
1 teaspoon	**vanilla paste**	5g
2 cups	**fresh blueberries**	296g
	Walnut Crumble (page 294), for topping (optional)	

1. Preheat the oven to 375°F. Prepare a muffin tin with paper liners.
2. Combine the milk and butter in a small saucepan. Heat over medium heat, stirring occasionally, until the butter is almost melted. Remove from the heat and let cool until the butter is completely melted and the mixture is lukewarm.
3. In a large bowl, whisk together the flour, granulated sugar, brown sugar, baking powder, and salt. Zest the lemon over the bowl.

Next page

BLUEBERRY MUFFINS, *continued*

4 Crack the eggs into a medium bowl. Add the vanilla and whisk to break up the yolks. Slowly whisk the milk mixture into the eggs.

5 Add the wet ingredients to the flour mixture and fold with a wooden spoon or silicone spatula until just a few streaks of flour remain. Gently fold in the blueberries.

6 For jumbo muffins, scoop ½ cup batter into each muffin cup. For standard muffins, scoop ¼ to ⅓ cup batter into each muffin cup. Top the muffins with walnut crumble, if using.

7 Bake standard muffins for 20 to 25 minutes and jumbo muffins for 25 to 30 minutes, until they are firm to the touch and a toothpick inserted in the middle comes out clean.

Muffins are best enjoyed the same day but can be stored overnight in an airtight container at room temperature. Revive tired muffins by splitting, toasting, and spreading with butter.

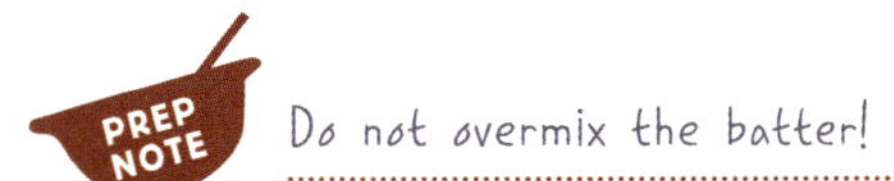

Grape-Walnut Muffins

Our friend Abby Schilling of Mick Klüg Farms and Schilling Family Farms recommends seeking out Canadice grapes for this unique recipe. Canadice grapes have a sweet flavor with a slight hint of spice. Plus, they're seedless, so you won't have to worry about picking out the seeds before you bake. Look for them at the farmers' markets around September.

Ingredients

Yield: 12 standard muffins or 6 jumbo muffins

¾ cup	**whole milk**	170g
½ cup (1 stick)	**unsalted butter**	113g
2 ⅓ cups	**all-purpose flour**	280g
¾ cup	**granulated sugar**	150g
¼ cup	**packed dark brown sugar**	53g
1 tablespoon	**baking powder**	12g
¾ teaspoon	**kosher salt**	2.25g
2	**large eggs**	100g
1 teaspoon	**vanilla paste**	5g
1½ cups	**grapes, halved**	225g
1 cup	**walnuts, roughly chopped**	120g

1. Preheat the oven to 375°F. Prepare a muffin tin with paper liners.
2. Combine the milk and butter in a small saucepan. Heat over medium heat, stirring occasionally, until the butter is almost melted. Remove from the heat and let cool until the butter is completely melted and the mixture is lukewarm.
3. In a large bowl, whisk together the flour, granulated sugar, brown sugar, baking powder, and salt.
4. Crack the eggs into a medium bowl. Add the vanilla and whisk to break up the yolks. Slowly whisk the milk mixture into the eggs.
5. Add the wet ingredients to the flour mixture and fold with a wooden spoon or silicone spatula until just a few streaks of flour remain. Gently fold in the grapes and walnuts.

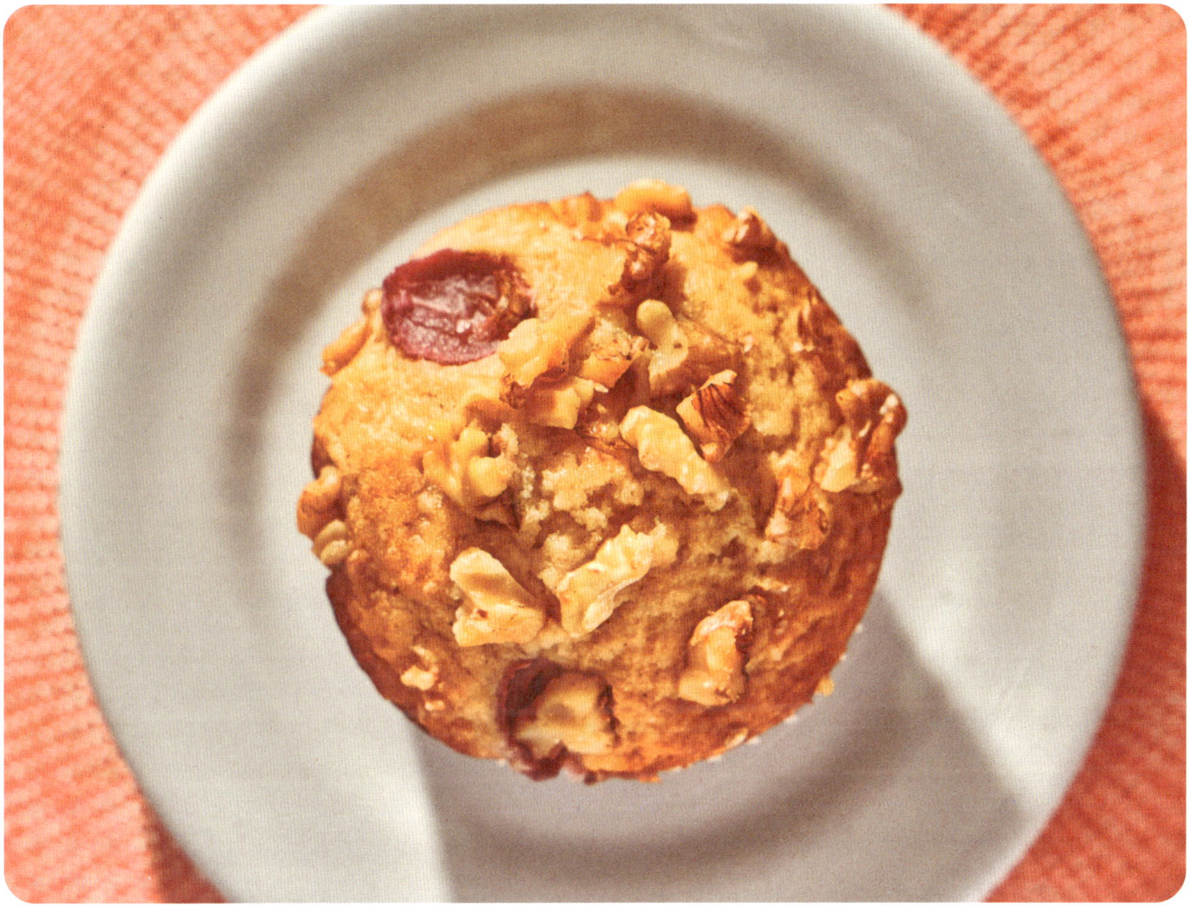

6 For jumbo muffins, scoop ½ cup batter into each muffin cup. For standard muffins, scoop ¼ to ⅓ cup batter into each muffin cup.

7 Bake standard muffins for 20 to 25 minutes and jumbo muffins for 25 to 30 minutes, until they are firm to the touch and a toothpick inserted in the middle comes out clean.

Muffins are best enjoyed the same day but can be stored overnight in an airtight container at room temperature. Revive tired muffins by splitting, toasting, and spreading with butter.

PREP NOTE Do not overmix the batter!

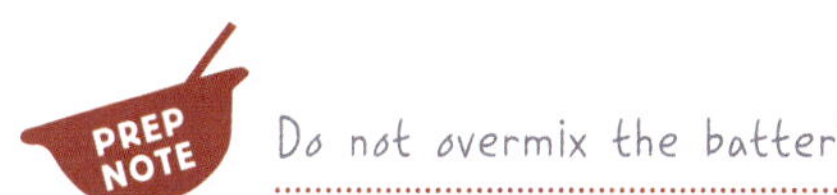

Orange-Chocolate Chip Muffins

After the hundreds of muffins we've tasted and tested in the shops over the years, this is still my husband's favorite. Adding a little orange zest transforms this kids' staple into an elegant pastry. It's especially good with a cup of coffee or strong black tea.

Ingredients

Yield: 12 standard muffins or 6 jumbo muffins

¾ cup	**whole milk**	170g
½ cup (1 stick)	**unsalted butter**	113g
2 ⅓ cups	**all-purpose flour**	280g
¾ cup	**granulated sugar**	150g
¼ cup	**packed dark brown sugar**	53g
1 tablespoon	**baking powder**	12g
¾ teaspoon	**kosher salt**	2.25g
	Grated zest of 1 orange	
2	**large eggs**	100g
1 teaspoon	**vanilla paste**	5g
1 cup	**chocolate chips**	170g
	Sanding sugar, for finishing (optional)	

1 Preheat the oven to 375°F. Prepare a muffin tin with paper liners.

2 Combine the milk and butter in a small saucepan. Heat over medium heat, stirring occasionally, until the butter is almost melted. Remove from the heat and let cool until the butter is completely melted and the mixture is lukewarm.

3 In a large bowl, whisk together the flour, granulated sugar, brown sugar, baking powder, and salt. Zest the orange over the bowl.

4 Crack the eggs into a medium bowl. Add the vanilla and whisk to break up the yolks. Slowly whisk the milk mixture into the eggs.

5 Add the wet ingredients to the flour mixture and fold with a wooden spoon or silicone spatula until just a few streaks of flour remain. Gently fold in the chocolate chips.

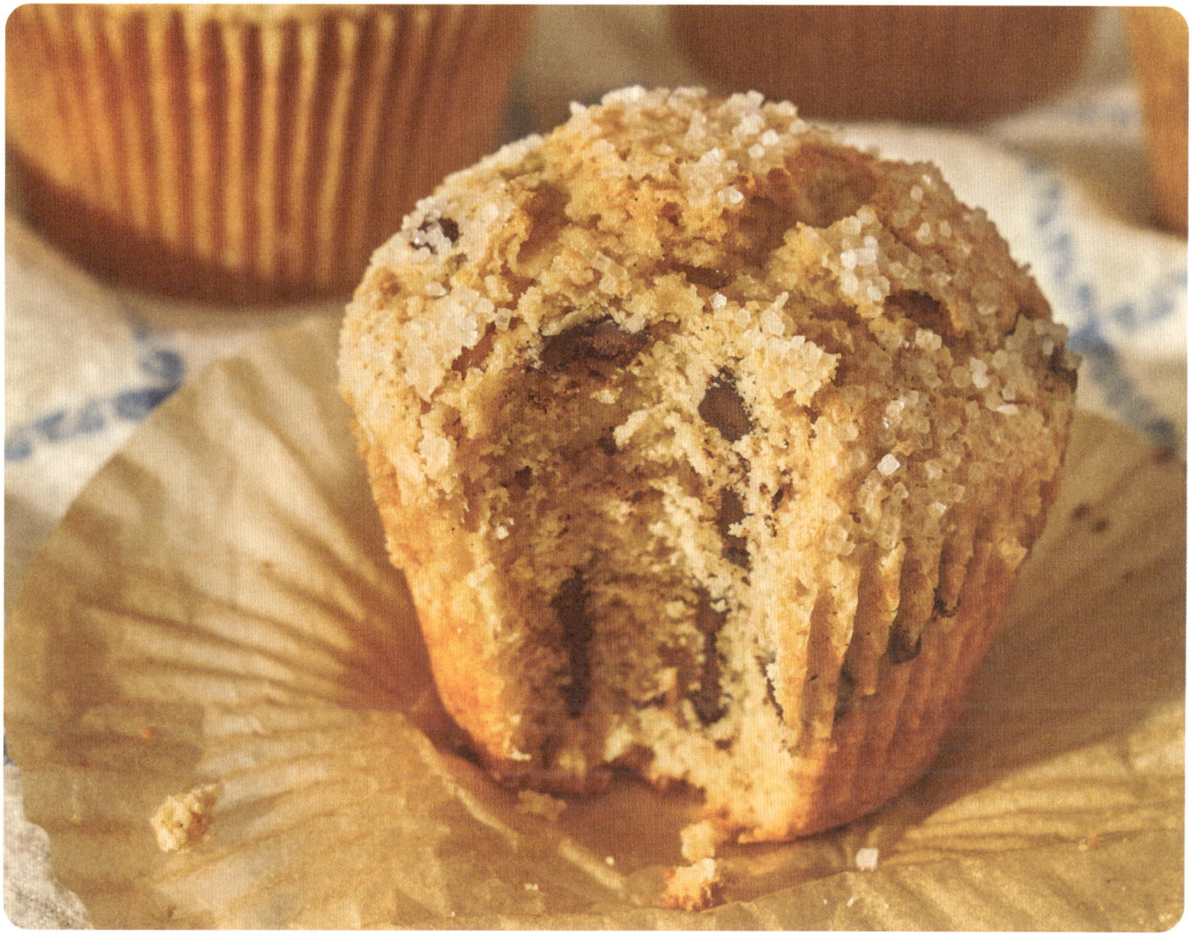

6 For jumbo muffins, scoop ½ cup batter into each muffin cup. For standard muffins, scoop ¼ to ⅓ cup batter into each muffin cup. Top the muffins with sanding sugar, if using.

7 Bake standard muffins for 20 to 25 minutes and jumbo muffins for 25 to 30 minutes, until they are firm to the touch and a toothpick inserted in the middle comes out clean.

Muffins are best enjoyed the same day but can be stored overnight in an airtight container at room temperature. Revive tired muffins by splitting, toasting, and spreading with butter.

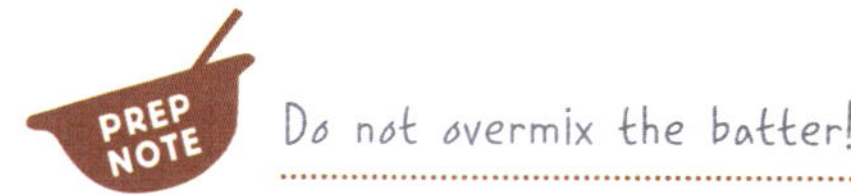

Strawberry Muffins

You can pair these strawberry muffins with all kinds of crumbles and glazes, but I like them best baked plain with just a sprinkling of sanding sugar. Skip the giant grocery store berries and seek out smaller, fragrant varieties from your local farmers' market or farm stand. Strawberry season is fleeting, so don't wait—get baking!

Ingredients

Yield: 12 standard muffins or 6 jumbo muffins

¾ cup	**whole milk**	170g
½ cup	**unsalted butter**	113g
2 ⅓ cups	**all-purpose flour**	280g
¾ cup	**granulated sugar**	150g
¼ cup	**packed dark brown sugar**	53g
1 tablespoon	**baking powder**	12g
¾ teaspoon	**kosher salt**	2.25g
2	**large eggs**	100g
1 teaspoon	**vanilla paste**	5g
2 cups	**halved (or quartered if large) strawberries**	336g
	Sanding sugar, for finishing (optional)	

1. Preheat the oven to 375°F. Prepare a muffin tin with paper liners.
2. Combine the milk and butter in a small saucepan. Heat over medium heat, stirring occasionally, until the butter is almost melted. Remove from the heat and let cool until the butter is completely melted and the mixture is lukewarm.
3. In a large bowl, whisk together the flour, granulated sugar, brown sugar, baking powder, and salt.
4. Crack the eggs into a medium bowl. Add the vanilla and whisk to break up the yolks. Slowly whisk the milk mixture into the eggs.
5. Add the wet ingredients to the flour mixture and fold with a wooden spoon or silicone spatula until just a few streaks of flour remain. Gently fold in the strawberries.

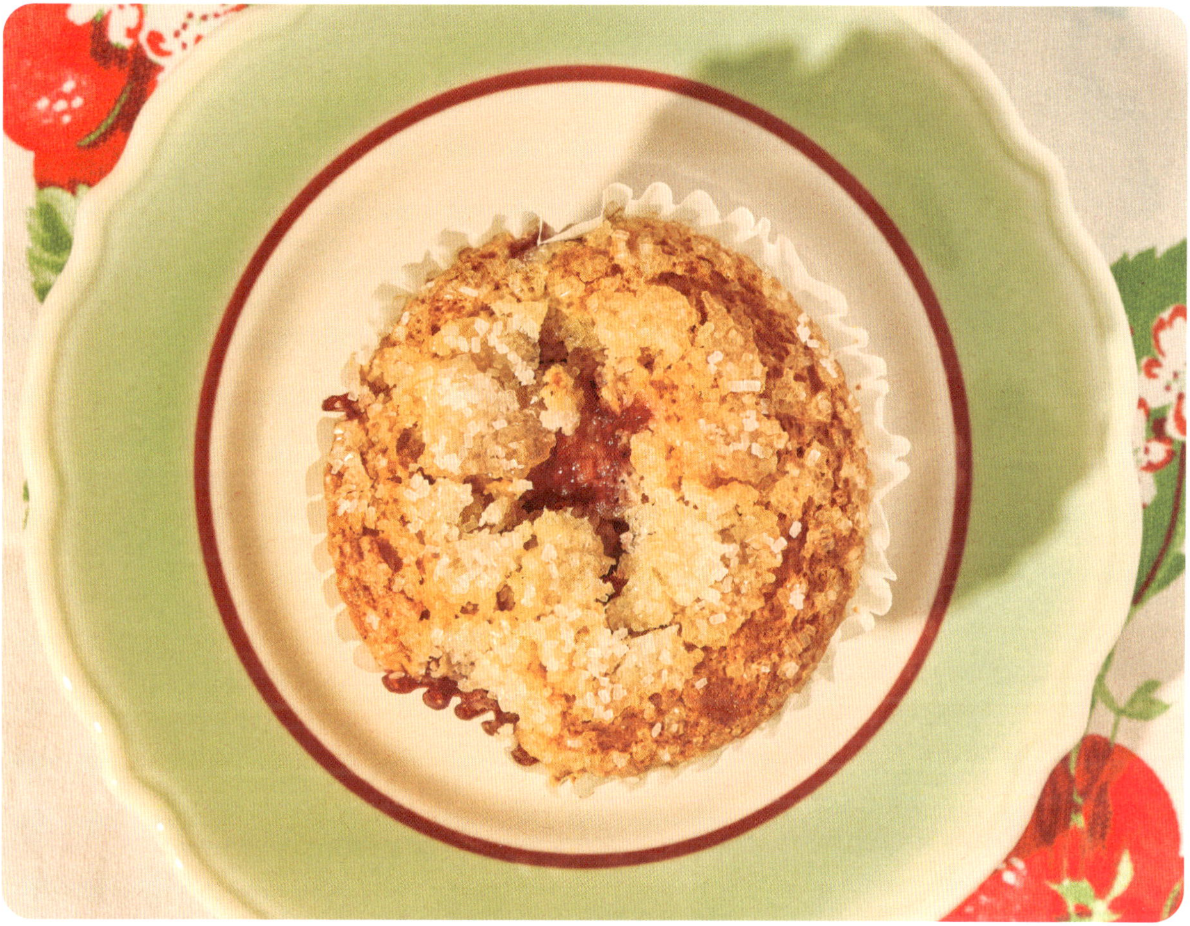

6 For jumbo muffins, scoop ½ cup batter into each muffin cup. For standard muffins, scoop ¼ to ⅓ cup batter into each muffin cup. Top the muffins with sanding sugar, if using.

7 Bake standard muffins for 20 to 25 minutes and jumbo muffins for 25 to 30 minutes, until they are firm to the touch and a toothpick inserted in the middle comes out clean.

Muffins are best enjoyed the same day but can be stored overnight in an airtight container at room temperature. Revive tired muffins by splitting, toasting, and spreading with butter.

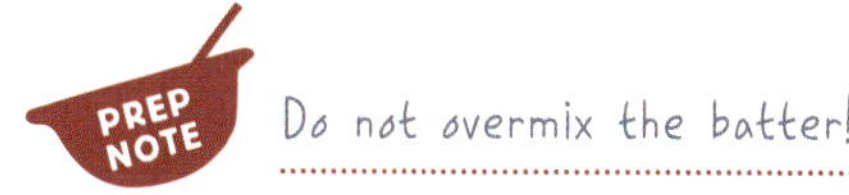

Banana Muffins

Somewhere, there is a banana going bad, if not on your kitchen counter, then on your neighbor's, your mother's, or the back of the grocery store display. For that, we have banana muffins. Luckily, you need truly terrible bananas to make the most delicious muffins. Choose bananas you wouldn't think of eating. They should have at the very least some black spots or streaks, but as long as they are not moldy or fermented, the blacker, the better.

Ingredients

Yield: 12 standard muffins or 6 jumbo muffins

1½ cups	**all-purpose flour**	180g
½ cup	**granulated sugar**	100g
¼ cup	**packed dark brown sugar**	53g
1 teaspoon	**baking soda**	6g
1 teaspoon	**baking powder**	4g
½ teaspoon	**kosher salt**	1.5g
¼ teaspoon	**ground cinnamon**	0.5g
⅛ teaspoon	**ground nutmeg**	0.3g
3 to 4	**medium ripe bananas, mashed**	340–450g total
⅓ cup	**unsalted butter, melted and cooled until lukewarm**	76g
1	**large egg**	50g
1 teaspoon	**vanilla paste**	5g
¾ cup	**chopped walnuts or chocolate chips (optional)**	90g

1. Preheat the oven to 375°F. Prepare a muffin tin with paper liners.
2. In a large bowl, whisk together the flour, granulated sugar, brown sugar, baking soda, baking powder, salt, cinnamon, and nutmeg.
3. In a large bowl, whisk together the mashed bananas, melted butter, egg, and vanilla until smooth.

Next page

BANANA MUFFINS, *continued*

4 Add the dry ingredients to the banana mixture and fold with a wooden spoon or silicone spatula until just a few streaks of flour remain. Gently fold in the chopped walnuts or chocolate chips, if using.

5 For jumbo muffins, scoop ½ cup batter into each muffin cup. For standard muffins, scoop ¼ to ⅓ cup batter into each muffin cup.

6 Bake standard muffins for 20 to 25 minutes and jumbo muffins for 25 to 30 minutes, until they are firm to the touch and a toothpick inserted in the middle comes out clean.

Store the muffin batter in the refrigerator for up to 3 days before baking. Store baked muffins in an airtight container at room temperature for up to 3 days. Revive tired muffins by splitting, toasting, and spreading with butter or whipped cream cheese (page 121).

Bananas getting away from you? *No problem! You can freeze overripe bananas for 2 to 3 months. I like to peel them in muffin-size batches into resealable freezer bags. Then, when I am ready to bake, I simply pull a bag out of the freezer and thaw it overnight in the refrigerator or under cold running water. The bananas will be a little watery, but it won't hurt the flavor or texture of the muffin.*

Chocolate-Chocolate Chip Muffins

Cocoa powder and brewed coffee give these muffins a deep, earthy chocolate flavor. If possible, use Dutch-processed cocoa powder. Dutching means the cocoa beans are soaked or washed in an alkaline solution before they are dried and ground, making the cocoa powder less bitter and intensely chocolatey. Droste, Hershey's Special Dark, and Ghirardelli Dutch-processed cocoa powders are available in most grocery stores. If you feel like splurging, look for Valrhona or Cacao Barry online or in specialty cooking stores.

Ingredients

Yield: 6 jumbo muffins or 12 standard muffins

1¾ cups	**all-purpose flour**	210g
¾ cups	**granulated sugar**	150g
2 tablespoons	**cocoa powder, preferably Dutch-processed**	12g
2 teaspoons	**baking powder**	8g
½ teaspoon	**baking soda**	2g
1 teaspoon	**kosher salt**	3g
1 cup	**whole milk**	240g
6 tablespoons	**canola oil**	84g
3 tablespoons	**strong brewed coffee, cooled**	45g
1	**large egg**	50g
2 teaspoons	**vanilla paste**	10g
¾ cup	**semisweet chocolate chips**	128g
	Sanding sugar, for finishing (optional)	

1 Preheat the oven to 375°F. Prepare a muffin tin with paper liners.

2 In a large bowl, whisk together the flour, granulated sugar, cocoa powder, baking powder, baking soda, and salt.

Next page

CHOCOLATE–CHOCOLATE CHIP MUFFINS, *continued*

3 In a small bowl, whisk together the milk, canola oil, coffee, egg, and vanilla paste. Whisk the coffee mixture into the flour mixture until most of the lumps are gone. Fold in the chocolate chips.

4 For jumbo muffins, scoop ½ cup batter into each muffin cup. For standard muffins, scoop ¼ to ⅓ cup batter into each muffin cup. Top the muffins with sanding sugar, if using.

5 Bake standard muffins for 20 to 25 minutes and jumbo muffins for 25 to 30 minutes, until they are firm to the touch and a toothpick inserted in the middle comes out clean.

Store baked muffins in an airtight container at room temperature for up to 3 days.

BLACK RASPBERRY–CHOCOLATE MUFFIN VARIATION: To make these into black raspberry–chocolate muffins (inspired by our favorite Graeter's ice cream flavor), reduce the chocolate chips to 1 cup and add 1 cup fresh black raspberries. We make these as soon as black raspberries come into season, in late June or early July. The season is short, usually just a few weeks, and they seldom show up in grocery stores, but if you are lucky, you can pick up a pint or two at a farmers' market.

Gingerbread Muffins

These muffins are pure holiday magic—not too sweet, with lots of warm wintery spices and pops of candied ginger. I'm a stickler for seasonality, but our baker Maria loves these so much, she's been known to put them on the menu in July on my days off. Hard to be mad, and customers love them too. If you don't see candied ginger in the supermarket, try an Asian grocer.

Ingredients

Yield: 12 standard muffins or 6 jumbo muffins

3 ½ cups	**all-purpose flour**	420g
2 ¼ cups	**packed dark brown sugar**	480g
1½ tablespoons	**ground ginger**	9g
1 tablespoon	**ground cinnamon**	6g
¾ teaspoon	**ground allspice**	1.5g
¾ teaspoon	**baking soda**	4.5g
¾ teaspoon	**kosher salt**	2.25g
1½ cups	**buttermilk**	340g
¾ cup (1½ sticks)	**unsalted butter, melted and cooled to room temperature**	170g
3	**large eggs**	150g
3 tablespoons	**chopped candied ginger**	30g
	Sanding sugar, for finishing (optional)	

1 Preheat the oven to 375°F. Prepare a muffin tin with paper liners.

2 In a large bowl, whisk together the flour, brown sugar, ginger, cinnamon, allspice, baking soda, and salt.

3 In a medium bowl, whisk together the buttermilk, melted butter, and eggs.

4 Add the wet ingredients to the flour mixture and fold with a wooden spoon or silicone spatula until just a few streaks of flour remain. Fold in the candied ginger.

5 For jumbo muffins, scoop ½ cup batter into each muffin cup. For standard muffins, scoop ¼ to ⅓ cup batter into each muffin cup. Top muffins with sanding sugar, if using.

6 Bake standard muffins for 20 to 25 minutes and jumbo muffins for 25 to 30 minutes, until they are firm to the touch and a toothpick inserted in the middle comes out clean.

Store the muffin batter in the fridge for up to 3 days before baking. Store baked muffins in an airtight container at room temperature for up to 2 days. Revive tired muffins by splitting, toasting, and spreading with butter.

Honey Corn Muffins

In its most basic form, this recipe makes a subtly sweet corn muffin with a satisfying cornmeal crunch and a crumb that's light enough to eat out of hand. Add a spoonful of jam or blueberry compote, and it makes our best-selling farmers' market muffin (see variation note). Add cheddar cheese and spices for a cornbread that's perfect with chili or black bean soup. Brushing the tops of warm muffins with honey gives them a pretty shine!

Ingredients

Yield: 12 standard muffins or 6 jumbo muffins

1 cup (2 sticks)	**unsalted butter, melted**	227g
¼ cup plus 2 tablespoons	**honey, divided**	126g
2 cups	**all-purpose flour**	240g
1 cup	**cornmeal**	138g
¾ cup	**sugar**	150g
2 teaspoons	**baking soda**	8g
1½ teaspoons	**baking powder**	6g
Pinch	**kosher salt**	
1 cup	**buttermilk**	227g
2	**large eggs**	100g

1 Preheat the oven to 375°F. Prepare a muffin tin with paper liners.

2 In a medium bowl, whisk together the melted butter and ¼ cup of the honey. Set aside until cooled to room temperature.

3 In a large bowl, whisk together the flour, cornmeal, sugar, baking soda, baking powder, and salt.

4 Whisk the buttermilk and eggs into the butter-honey mixture. Fold the butter mixture into the cornmeal mixture until just combined.

Next page

HONEY CORN MUFFINS, *continued*

5 For jumbo muffins, scoop ½ cup batter into each muffin cup. For standard muffins, scoop ¼ to ⅓ cup batter into each muffin cup.

6 Bake standard muffins for 20 to 25 minutes and jumbo muffins for 25 to 30 minutes, until they are firm to the touch and a toothpick inserted in the middle comes out clean.

7 Brush the warm muffins with the remaining 2 tablespoons honey.

Store the muffin batter in the fridge for up to 3 days before baking. Store baked muffins in an airtight container at room temperature for up to 3 days. Revive tired muffins by splitting, toasting, and spreading with butter and honey.

JAM-FILLED CORN MUFFIN VARIATION: These corn muffins also work well with a surprise jam or fruit compote center. Our farmers' market customers love these muffins filled with sweet blueberry compote or housemade raspberry jam, but don't hesitate to try something more adventurous like tomato or peach jalapeño, especially if you are serving them with a salad or something savory. Simply follow these instructions:

For standard-sized muffins, scoop ¼ cup batter into each muffin cup. For jumbo muffins, scoop ½ cup batter into each muffin cup. Dip a tablespoon into a cup or bowl of ice water and make an indentation in the batter. Repeat, dipping the spoon into the ice water between each muffin. Fill each indentation with 1 teaspoon jam or compote for standard muffins and 1 tablespoon jam or compote for jumbo muffins. For standard muffins, cover the jam with 1 tablespoon batter. For jumbo muffins, cover the jam with 2 tablespoons batter. Spread the batter to the edges of the muffin cup with your fingers, the back of a spoon, or an offset spatula. It's OK if some of the jam peeks through. Bake as directed in the main recipe.

Honey Cheddar Cornbread

This is our Honey Corn Muffins recipe (page 45) transformed into a sweet, cheesy, spicy, smoky cornbread. Spread the batter in a quarter sheet pan, a baking pan, a 9-inch cast-iron skillet, cornbread molds, or muffin tins. If you don't have smoked paprika, you can use regular paprika or leave it out, but it is worth your time to track some down. Once you have it, you'll find yourself reaching for it again and again. I like to rub it on broiled salmon and sprinkle it on baked chicken. We even add it to the crumble topping for our Whiskey Caramel Apple Pie for some smoky sophistication.

Ingredients

Yield: 6–8 generous servings

1 cup (2 sticks)	**unsalted butter, melted**	227g
2 tablespoons	**honey**	42g
2 cups	**all-purpose flour**	240g
1 cup	**cornmeal**	138g
¾ cup	**sugar**	150g
2 tablespoons	**ground mustard**	12g
2 teaspoons	**baking soda**	8g
1½ teaspoons	**baking powder**	6g
1 teaspoon	**smoked paprika**	2.3g
¼ teaspoon	**kosher salt**	0.75g
⅛ teaspoon	**ground cayenne pepper**	0.3g
⅛ teaspoon	**freshly ground black pepper**	0.3g
1 cup	**buttermilk**	227g
2	**large eggs**	100g
2 cups	**shredded cheddar cheese**	226g
2 tablespoons	**honey or hot honey, for topping (optional)**	42g

Next page

HONEY CHEDDAR CORNBREAD, *continued*

1. Preheat the oven to 375°F. Spray a 9⅝ × 13-inch rimmed baking sheet or 9 × 13-inch baking pan with cooking spray. If you plan on unmolding the cornbread, line the sprayed pan with parchment and spray the parchment as well.
2. In a medium bowl, whisk together the melted butter and honey. Set aside until cooled to room temperature.
3. In a large bowl, whisk together the flour, cornmeal, sugar, mustard, baking soda, baking powder, paprika, salt, cayenne, and black pepper.
4. Whisk the buttermilk and eggs into the butter-honey mixture. Fold the butter mixture into the cornmeal mixture until just combined. Fold in the cheddar cheese.
5. Spread batter in the prepared pan.
6. Bake for 20 minutes, turning the pan halfway through, or until the top is firm and the cornbread starts to pull away from the sides of the pan.
7. Brush the top of the warm cornbread with the hot honey, if using.

Store cornbread batter in the fridge for up to 3 days before baking. Store baked cornbread in an airtight container, or wrapped with aluminum foil or plastic film, at room temperature for up to 3 days.

Morning Glory Muffins

When Pam McKinstry dreamed up this muffin at her Nantucket Island Morning Glory Café in 1978, they were an immediate hit. In 1981, she graciously published the recipe in *Gourmet* magazine in response to reader requests, and the rest is breakfast pastry history. They were soon a staple in "crunchy" coffee houses across the country, including the Runcible Spoon in Bloomington, Indiana, where I probably ate as many as I baked. They really are glorious, in the morning or anytime. I like to split them in half, spread them with cream cheese, and call them lunch. I'm almost certain we used McKinstry's original recipe, which calls for the addition of frozen pineapple chunks. Lots of folks have published their versions over the years. Ours is a pretty straightforward recipe that takes advantage of ingredients we always have on hand. Feel free to get creative and dream up a version of your own. I'm sure Chef McKinstry would not mind.

Ingredients

Yield: 12 standard muffins or 6 jumbo muffins

2 cups	**all-purpose flour**	240g
1¼ cups	**sugar**	250g
2 teaspoons	**baking soda**	8g
2 teaspoons	**ground cinnamon**	5g
½ teaspoon	**kosher salt**	1.5g
3	**large eggs**	150g
1 cup	**canola oil**	218g
1 tablespoon	**vanilla paste**	15g
1⅓ cups	**peeled and grated carrots**	170g
1 cup	**peeled, cored, and grated apples**	115g
⅓ cup	**sweetened coconut flakes**	32g
	Grated zest of 1 orange	
½ cup	**raisins**	75g
½ cup	**roughly chopped walnuts or pecans (optional)**	60g

Next page

MORNING GLORY MUFFINS, *continued*

1. Preheat the oven to 375°F. Prepare a muffin tin with paper liners.
2. In a large bowl, whisk together the flour, sugar, baking soda, cinnamon, and salt.
3. Crack the eggs into a medium bowl and whisk briefly to break up the yolks. Stir in the canola oil and vanilla paste. Add the carrots, apples, and coconut flakes and stir gently until the shredded ingredients are evenly distributed. Zest the orange over the bowl.
4. Gently fold the carrot-apple mixture into the flour mixture until mostly combined. Stir in the raisins and optional nuts.
5. For jumbo muffins, scoop ½ cup batter into each muffin cup. For standard muffins, scoop ¼ to ⅓ cup batter into each muffin cup.
6. Bake standard muffins for 20 to 25 minutes and jumbo muffins for 25 to 30 minutes, until they are firm to the touch and a toothpick inserted in the middle comes out clean.

Store the muffin batter in the refrigerator for up to 3 days before baking. Store baked muffins in an airtight container at room temperature for up to 3 days. Revive tired muffins by splitting, toasting, and spreading with butter, cream cheese, or honey.

PREP NOTE

Golden raisins have a lighter, brighter flavor than traditional dark raisins. If traditional raisins aren't your thing, give them a try. I like to use a combination of both for a more complex flavor and to make the muffins look more interesting.

Olive Oil Orange-Cardamom Muffins

There is always a trade-off when deciding whether to use oil or butter as the fat of choice in a muffin recipe. Oil-based muffins, like these, are generally moister and have a more delicate crumb than their butter-based brethren. Thanks to the oil, they also stay fresher longer. Unfortunately, they usually call for a bland, flavorless oil, whereas butter tastes like butter! The genius of this recipe is that an intensely flavored olive oil adds to the taste of the muffin, and the finer crumb is perfect with the subtle hints of almond and cognac. Our longtime, unflappable pie slinger, Alyssa, developed this recipe to make the most of some ingredients we always have on hand.

Ingredients

Yield: 12 standard muffins or 6 jumbo muffins

2½ cups	**all-purpose flour**	300g
1⅓ cups	**sugar**	266g
1¼ teaspoons	**ground cardamom**	3g
1 teaspoon	**kosher salt**	3g
½ teaspoon	**baking powder**	2g
½ teaspoon	**baking soda**	2g
1½ cups	**olive oil**	318g
1 cup plus 2 tablespoons	**whole milk**	255g
2½ tablespoons	**orange juice**	37g
2 tablespoons	**cognac**	30g
2	**large eggs**	100g
1½ teaspoons	**almond extract**	6g
	Grated zest of 1 orange	
1 recipe	**Orange Glaze (page 291), for finishing**	

Next page

OLIVE OIL ORANGE-CARDAMOM MUFFINS, *continued*

1 Preheat the oven to 375°F. Prepare a muffin tin with paper liners.

2 In a large bowl, whisk together the flour, sugar, cardamom, salt, baking powder, and baking soda.

3 In a medium bowl, whisk together the olive oil, milk, orange juice, cognac, eggs, and almond extract. Zest the orange into the oil mixture. Fold the oil mixture into the flour mixture until just combined.

4 For jumbo muffins, scoop ½ cup batter into each muffin cup. For standard muffins, scoop ¼ to ⅓ cup batter into each muffin cup.

5 Bake standard muffins for 20 to 25 minutes and jumbo muffins for 25 to 30 minutes, until they are firm to the touch and a toothpick inserted in the middle comes out clean.

6 Set the muffins aside until they are cool enough to remove from the pan. Transfer to a wire rack to cool completely. When cool, glaze the muffins.

Store the muffin batter in the refrigerator for up to 2 days before baking. Store baked muffins in an airtight container at room temperature for up to 3 days. Revive tired muffins by splitting, toasting, and spreading with butter or cream cheese.

Always zest citrus directly over the other ingredients in a recipe and not into a separate container. You want to capture both the citrus peel and the citrus oil that falls from the fruit as you zest it.

Peanut Butter Muffins

If you like peanut butter, you'll love these muffins. They are just sweet enough to be a treat but substantial enough to power your morning. Homogenized commercial peanut butter, like Skippy or Jif, works best for baking since the oils don't separate, and the uniform texture makes them easy to mix in your batter. We use creamy-style peanut butter in the shop, but you can substitute crunchy if you prefer. I use a whisk to fold the dry ingredients into the thinner peanut butter–canola oil mixture. It helps break up any lumps without overmixing.

Ingredients

Yield: 12 standard muffins or 6 jumbo muffins

MUFFINS

¾ cup	**peanut butter**	192g
½ cup	**honey**	170g
2	**large eggs**	100g
½ cup	**canola oil**	109g
1 cup	**whole milk**	227g
1 teaspoon	**vanilla paste**	5g
1½ cups	**all-purpose flour**	180g
½ cup	**granulated sugar**	100g
1½ teaspoons	**baking powder**	6g
½ teaspoon	**kosher salt**	1.5g

PEANUT STREUSEL

1 cup	**dry-roasted peanuts, chopped**	146g
½ cup	**all-purpose flour**	60g
3 tablespoons	**packed dark brown sugar**	40g
2 tablespoons	**granulated sugar**	25g
Pinch	**kosher salt**	
¼ cup (½ stick)	**unsalted butter, melted**	57g

Save time and effort by bringing the ingredients to room temperature before mixing.

Next page

PEANUT BUTTER MUFFINS, *continued*

1. Preheat the oven to 375°F. Prepare a muffin tin with paper liners.
2. Measure the peanut butter into a large bowl.
3. Measure the honey into a microwave-safe dish and heat for 30 seconds. Stir. Repeat in 10-second intervals until the honey is warm but not hot. Whisk the honey into the peanut butter.
4. Add the eggs one at a time, whisking after each addition. Slowly whisk in the canola oil, milk, and vanilla paste and keep whisking until the oil is incorporated.
5. In a small bowl, whisk together the flour, granulated sugar, baking powder, and salt.
6. Using a whisk, fold the flour mixture into the peanut butter mixture. The batter will be thin.
7. To make the peanut streusel, combine the peanuts, flour, brown sugar, granulated sugar, and salt in a small bowl and mix well. Add the melted butter and rub the ingredients together with your fingers until it is crumbly.
8. For jumbo muffins, scoop ½ cup batter into each muffin cup. For standard muffins, scoop ¼ to ⅓ cup batter into each muffin cup. Top jumbo muffins with ¼ cup peanut streusel. Top standard muffins with 2 tablespoons peanut streusel.
9. Bake standard muffins for 25 to 30 minutes and jumbo muffins for 30 to 35 minutes, until they are firm to the touch and a toothpick inserted in the middle comes out clean.

Store the muffin batter in the refrigerator for up to 2 days before baking. Store baked muffins in an airtight container at room temperature for up to 3 days. Revive a tired muffin by splitting, toasting, and spreading with butter, honey, or grape jelly.

Persimmon Muffins

Diospyros virginiana, the botanical name for the American persimmon tree, loosely translates to "fruit of the gods." The way Hoosiers, myself included, talk about persimmons, you'd believe it! In the fall, persimmon trees produce a burnt orange–colored fruit the size of a plum that tastes like a cross between a pumpkin and an apricot with a bit of honey and allspice thrown in, but that's only after it ripens into a pudding-y blob and falls off the tree. Unripe persimmons are so tannic and acidic that they'll pucker your lips and leave you with cotton mouth. It's a wonder we learned to eat them at all. In southern Indiana, they are traditionally baked into cookies, pies, candies, and puddings, though I have also tried persimmon wine and persimmon milkshakes. The rich persimmon pulp lends itself to moist, flavorful muffins that are hearty enough to stand up to the addition of nuts and dried fruit if you like.

You'll need to buy the fruit directly from a small farm to try the real deal. The persimmons you find in grocery stores are an Asian variety that can be shipped while they are still green. To me, the flavor just doesn't compare. American persimmon growers string nets under the trees to catch the falling ripened fruit, then scoop out the pulp and sell it frozen. It is a good idea to keep the fruit frozen until you plan to use it. Thaw it in the refrigerator overnight or under cool running water. Thaw only what you plan to use and refreeze any unused portions.

Next page

PERSIMMON MUFFINS, *continued*

Ingredients

Yield: 12 standard muffins or 6 jumbo muffins

2 cups	**all-purpose flour**	240g
2 cups	**sugar**	400g
2 teaspoons	**baking powder**	8g
1½ teaspoons	**ground cinnamon**	4g
½ teaspoon	**baking soda**	2g
½ teaspoon	**kosher salt**	1.5g
½ teaspoon	**ground nutmeg**	1.1g
¼ teaspoon	**ground mace**	~0.5g
1 cup	**frozen persimmon pulp, thawed**	245g
	Grated zest of 2 oranges	
½ cup (1 stick)	**unsalted butter, melted**	113g
½ cup	**whole milk**	113g
2	**large eggs**	100g
1 tablespoon	**vanilla paste**	15g
1 cup	**dried cherries**	120g
1 cup	**roughly chopped pecans**	120g

1. Preheat the oven to 375°F. Prepare a muffin tin with paper liners.
2. In a large bowl, whisk together the flour, sugar, baking powder, cinnamon, baking soda, salt, nutmeg, and mace.
3. Use a bowl scraper or a silicone spatula to press the persimmon pulp through a fine-mesh sieve into a medium bowl. Zest the oranges over the persimmon pulp. Whisk the melted butter into the persimmon pulp, followed by the milk, eggs, and vanilla paste.
4. Gently fold the persimmon mixture into the flour mixture until almost combined. You should still see streaks of flour. Fold in the dried cherries and pecans until just combined.
5. For jumbo muffins, scoop ½ cup batter into each muffin cup. For standard muffins, scoop ¼ to ⅓ cup batter into each muffin cup.
6. Bake standard muffins for 20 to 25 minutes and jumbo muffins for 25 to 30 minutes, until they are firm to the touch and a toothpick inserted in the middle comes out clean.

Store the muffin batter in the refrigerator for up to 2 days before baking. Store baked muffins in an airtight container at room temperature for up to 3 days. Revive a tired muffin by splitting, toasting, and spreading with butter.

Pumpkin Muffins with Dried Cherries or Chocolate Chips

These are some of my all-time favorite muffins. The combination of pumpkin and dried cherries is unexpected, and the sweet-tart cherry flavor pops, making the pumpkin more pumpkiny and brightening up the whole muffin. You can always substitute chocolate chips, because who doesn't like pumpkin and chocolate? Kids especially make a beeline for the pastry case whenever we have them. At the shop, we top the muffins with coarse-grained sugar before they go into the oven, but that's mostly for looks. They're fantastic as is or with a light dusting of powdered sugar once they cool.

Ingredients

Yield: 12 standard muffins or 6 jumbo muffins

2½ cups	**all-purpose flour**	300g
2¼ cups	**granulated sugar**	450g
1½ teaspoons	**baking soda**	6g
1⅛ teaspoons	**kosher salt**	3.4g
¾ teaspoon	**ground cinnamon**	2g
½ teaspoon	**ground cloves**	1g
½ teaspoon	**ground ginger**	1g
1½ cups	**canned pumpkin puree**	368g
¾ cup	**canola oil**	164g
½ cup	**buttermilk**	113g
3	**large eggs**	150g
1 teaspoon	**vanilla paste**	5g
1 cup	**dried cherries or chocolate chips**	120g
	Sanding sugar or 1 recipe Popped Pumpkin Seeds (page 289), for topping (optional)	

Next page

PUMPKIN MUFFINS WITH DRIED CHERRIES OR CHOCOLATE CHIPS, *continued*

1 Preheat the oven to 375°F. Prepare a muffin tin with paper liners.

2 In a large bowl, whisk together the flour, granulated sugar, baking soda, salt, cinnamon, cloves, and ginger.

3 In a medium bowl, whisk together the pumpkin puree, canola oil, buttermilk, eggs, and vanilla.

4 Fold the pumpkin mixture into the flour mixture until it is almost combined. You should still see streaks of flour. Add the dried cherries or chocolate chips and mix until just combined.

5 For jumbo muffins, scoop ½ cup batter into each muffin cup. For standard muffins, scoop ¼ to ⅓ cup batter into each muffin cup. Top with optional sanding sugar or popped pumpkin seeds, if using.

6 Bake standard muffins for 20 to 25 minutes and jumbo muffins for 25 to 30 minutes, until they are firm to the touch and a toothpick inserted in the middle comes out clean.

Store the muffin batter in the refrigerator for up to 3 days before baking. Store baked muffins in an airtight container at room temperature for up to 3 days. Revive tired muffins by splitting, toasting, and spreading with butter or whipped cream cheese (page 121).

PUMPKIN CREAM CHEESE MUFFIN VARIATION: I admit it. Our pumpkin cream cheese muffin recipe was inspired by the popularity of a certain muffin at a certain coffee shop chain that everyone raves about. Could we make it better? I think so, but it is not exactly a fair fight. We have the luxury of baking these fresh every day, and so do you. We "popped" the pumpkin seed garnish and added as much cream cheese filling as the muffin would hold. Best of all, it combines three recipes in our repertoire to make something new. It is a good idea to make the cream cheese filling a day ahead and let it firm up in the fridge overnight. For the best muffin-to-filling ratio, make these muffins jumbo-sized. Scoop ½ cup batter into each jumbo muffin cup, then dip a tablespoon into a cup or bowl of ice water and make an indentation in the center of the batter. Repeat, dipping the spoon into the ice water between each muffin. Fill the indentation with 2 tablespoons of Cream Cheese Filling (page 292). Top with 2 tablespoons of muffin batter. Spread the batter to the edges of the muffin cup with your fingers, the back of a spoon, or an offset spatula. It's OK if some of the cream cheese peeks through. Top each muffin with Popped Pumpkin Seeds (page 289). Bake for 30 to 35 minutes, until the muffins are domed in the center and the tops look matte and dry. The center of the muffins may fall a bit as they cool.

Pumpkin Cream Cheese Muffin Variation

Rainbow Carrot Cake Muffins

Chicago winters are long, cold, and dark. One bright spot is the boxes of fresh produce Liz Werp delivers every Thursday night from her family's farm in northern Michigan. Werp Farms grows flowers, greens, herbs, and all kinds of vegetables year-round in wood-fired greenhouses. I developed this recipe to take advantage of their sweet white, yellow, purple, and orange winter carrots and baked the cream cheese icing right in to make them easy to transport. If you can't find rainbow carrots, any color will work. Just look for smaller, younger carrots—they are sweeter and less woody. Anything from a reputable farmers' market should be fine. At the grocery store, look for organic carrots and/or carrots that still have the stems and leaves attached. The whole wheat pastry flour in this recipe adds a hearty texture and a subtle nuttiness that complements the sweetness of the carrots. But don't worry if you don't have any on hand—you can always substitute all-purpose flour.

Ingredients

Yield: 12 standard muffins or 6 jumbo muffins

2¼ cups	**peeled and grated carrots**	300g
3	**large eggs**	150g
¾ cup	**canola oil**	164g
½ cup	**sour cream**	120g
1½ teaspoons	**vanilla paste**	7.5g
1 cup	**whole wheat pastry flour**	120g
1 cup	**all-purpose flour**	120g
1½ cups	**packed dark brown sugar**	320g
1½ teaspoons	**baking powder**	6g
1½ teaspoons	**ground cinnamon**	4g
1 teaspoon	**ground ginger**	2g
¾ teaspoon	**baking soda**	3g
¾ teaspoon	**kosher salt**	2.25g
½ teaspoon	**ground nutmeg**	1g
6 tablespoons	**Cream Cheese Filling (page 292)**	
2 tablespoons	**honey**	35g

Next page

RAINBOW CARROT CAKE MUFFINS, *continued*

1. Preheat the oven to 375°F. Prepare a muffin tin with paper liners.
2. In a large bowl, combine the grated carrots, eggs, canola oil, sour cream, and vanilla paste and mix well. Make sure the carrots are separated and evenly distributed. I like putting on gloves and using my hands, but a silicone spatula or wooden spoon works, too.
3. In a medium bowl, whisk together the the whole wheat flour, all-purpose flour, brown sugar, baking powder, cinnamon, ginger, baking soda, salt, and nutmeg. Fold the flour mixture into the carrot mixture until combined.
4. For jumbo muffins, spoon ¼ cup batter into the prepared muffin cups. Top with 1 tablespoon cream cheese filling and 1 teaspoon honey. Cover with another ½ cup batter. Smooth the batter to the edge of the muffin cups if necessary. For standard muffins, spoon 2 tablespoons batter into the prepared muffin cups. Top with 1½ teaspoons cream cheese filling and ½ teaspoon honey. Cover with another 2 tablespoons batter. Smooth the batter to the edge of the muffin cups if necessary.
5. Bake standard muffins for 20 to 25 minutes and jumbo muffins for 30 to 35 minutes, until they are firm to the touch. They will bake off dark as the sugar in the carrots caramelizes. The whole wheat pastry flour also gives them a darker color. If the tops of the muffins are browning too much, place a baking sheet on the rack above them in the oven or lay a sheet of aluminum foil loosely over the muffin tin.

Rise & Shine Muffins

Yup, it's another riff on the legendary Morning Glory Muffins (page 49)! I developed this recipe years ago for an event with Pilot Light, a food education nonprofit, and Chicago Public Schools. The assignment was to highlight local, seasonal produce and have the kids taste something they might not have tried before. I am not a big fan of "tricking" kids into eating their veggies. I did, however, give zucchini a little glow-up with these muffins! First off, I added sugar and local honey for sweetness. The honey, apple, and zucchini bring seasonal flavor while locking in moisture, and the whole wheat pastry flour adds a hearty texture and nutty flavor. I top them with some large-grain sanding sugar for attention-grabbing sparkle. We make these in late summer/early fall when our farmers harvest their first fall apples but are still overrun with summer zucchini. Feel free to substitute lightly toasted sunflower and/or pumpkin seeds for the optional nuts.

Ingredients

Yield: 12 standard muffins or 6 jumbo muffins

3 cups	**whole wheat pastry flour**	360g
1½ cups	**sugar**	300g
1 tablespoon	**baking soda**	12g
1 tablespoon	**ground cinnamon**	8g
¾ teaspoon	**kosher salt**	2.25g
3	**large eggs**	150g
1 cup	**canola oil**	218g
¼ cup	**honey**	85g
1 tablespoon	**vanilla paste**	15g
1¼ cups	**peeled, cored, and grated apples**	150g
1 cup	**peeled and grated carrots**	135g
1 cup	**grated zucchini**	135g
⅓ cup	**sweetened coconut flakes**	32g
	Grated zest of 1 orange	
¾ cup	**dried cherries, raisins, or other dried fruit (optional)**	90g
¾ cup	**roughly chopped walnuts or pecans (optional)**	90g

Next page

RISE & SHINE MUFFINS, *continued*

1 Preheat the oven to 375°F. Prepare a muffin tin with paper liners.

2 In a large bowl, whisk together the flour, sugar, baking soda, cinnamon, and salt.

3 Crack the eggs into a medium bowl and whisk briefly to break up the yolks. Stir in the canola oil, honey, and vanilla paste. Add the apples, carrots, zucchini, and coconut flakes and stir gently until the shredded ingredients are evenly distributed. Zest the orange over the bowl.

4 Gently fold the carrot-zucchini mixture into the flour mixture until mostly combined. Stir in the optional raisins and nuts, if using.

5 For jumbo muffins, scoop ½ cup batter into each muffin cup. For standard muffins, scoop ¼ to ⅓ cup batter into each muffin cup.

6 Bake standard muffins for 20 to 25 minutes and jumbo muffins for 25 to 30 minutes, until they are firm to the touch and a toothpick inserted in the middle comes out clean.

Store the muffin batter in the refrigerator for up to 3 days before baking. Store baked muffins in an airtight container at room temperature for up to 3 days. Revive tired muffins by splitting, toasting, and spreading with butter, cream cheese, or honey.

Sweet Potato Muffins

I don't add any spices to these muffins, just a little salt and pepper, so the earthy natural sweetness of the sweet potatoes shines through. We roast the sweet potatoes in the oven until they are soft to concentrate the flavor, then puree them in a food processor and push them through a fine-mesh sieve. A food mill or ricer also works. So does mashing the potatoes in a mixer or by hand. If you don't mind an occasional nugget of sweet potato in your muffin, you can skip the sieve and cut down on the prep time.

Ingredients

Yield: 12 standard muffins or 6 jumbo muffins

3	**medium sweet potatoes, well scrubbed**	450–600g
¾ cup	**canola oil**	164g
3	**large eggs**	150g
½ cup	**buttermilk**	113g
1 teaspoon	**vanilla paste**	5g
	Grated zest of ½ orange	
2½ cups	**all-purpose flour**	300g
2¼ cups	**granulated sugar**	450g
1½ teaspoons	**baking soda**	6g
1 teaspoon	**kosher salt**	3g
1 teaspoon	**freshly ground black pepper**	2g
	Sanding sugar, for finishing (optional)	

1 Preheat the oven to 375°F. Prepare a muffin tin with paper liners.

2 Prick the sweet potatoes all over with a fork. Place on a rimmed baking sheet and bake for 45 to 60 minutes, until very soft. Set aside until cool enough to handle, but no longer than 2 hours (see sidebar).

Next page

SWEET POTATO MUFFINS, *continued*

3 Cut the sweet potatoes in half and scoop the flesh into the bowl of a food processor, stand mixer, food mill, or potato ricer. Process or mash potatoes until smooth. (You can also mash the potatoes by hand.) If desired, press the sweet potato puree through a fine-mesh sieve for a smoother texture.

4 Measure 1½ cups of the mashed sweet potatoes into a large bowl. (Reserve the rest in the refrigerator for another use.) Whisk in the canola oil until well combined, then add the eggs, buttermilk, and vanilla, whisking well after each addition. Zest the orange over the sweet potato mixture.

5 In a medium bowl, whisk together the flour, granulated sugar, baking soda, salt, and pepper.

6 Add the flour mixture to the sweet potato mixture and whisk to combine.

7 For jumbo muffins, scoop ½ cup batter into each muffin cup. For standard muffins, scoop ¼ to ⅓ cup batter into each muffin cup. Top with sanding sugar, if using.

8 Bake standard muffins for 25 to 30 minutes and jumbo muffins for 30 to 35 minutes, until they are firm to the touch and a toothpick inserted in the middle comes out clean.

Store the muffin batter in the fridge for up to 3 days before baking. Store baked muffins in an airtight container in the refrigerator for up to 2 days. Revive tired muffins by splitting, toasting, and spreading with butter.

BAKING AND STORING POTATOES

You don't need to wrap sweet potatoes or any kind of potatoes in aluminum foil to bake them, but if you do, be sure to remove the foil as soon as the potatoes come out of the oven. Wrapping a potato in foil keeps oxygen from reaching it and can allow the group of bacteria that causes botulism, a nasty neurotoxin, to grow. Botulism is rare but can be fatal, especially if left untreated. The USDA advises that cooked potatoes be served immediately or stored in the refrigerator after 2 hours. The sweet potato puree will keep in the refrigerator for up to 3 days or in the freezer for up to 2 weeks. Thaw in the refrigerator overnight before use.

Oil-Based Muffin Base

Don't be put off by the clunky name. This recipe makes an excellent and handy muffin batter that bakes up into beautiful round-top, cake-like muffins with a delicate crumb and subtle hints of vanilla and lemon zest. The real magic? You can prepare it in advance and store it in the refrigerator for up to a week. We love using it as the base for our Lemon Poppy Seed Muffins, but the possibilities are endless—see our chart of variations on page 71. You can mix in fresh fruit or fruit compotes to customize the flavor on the fly. The use of oil in this recipe inhibits gluten formation, allowing you to mix it by hand or in a stand mixer without the need for careful folding of ingredients.

Ingredients

Yield: 12 standard muffins or 6 jumbo muffins

¼ cup (½ stick)	**unsalted butter, melted and cooled to room temperature**	57g
¼ cup	**canola oil**	55g
1½ cups	**sugar**	300g
2½ cups	**all-purpose flour**	300g
1 tablespoon	**baking powder**	12g
¾ teaspoon	**kosher salt**	2.25g
	Grated zest of ½ lemon	
2	**large eggs**	100g
1 cup	**whole milk**	227g
1 teaspoon	**vanilla paste**	5g
	Optional additions (see page 71)	

1. Preheat the oven to 375°F. Prepare a muffin tin with paper liners.
2. In a large bowl, mix the melted butter, canola oil, and sugar with a wooden spoon or silicone spatula until combined. (Alternatively, use a stand mixer fitted with the paddle attachment and beat on medium speed.)
3. In a medium bowl, whisk together the flour, baking powder, and salt. Zest the lemon over the flour mixture.
4. Crack the eggs into another medium bowl. Whisk in the milk and vanilla paste.

5 Alternate adding the flour mixture and egg mixture to the oil mixture, beginning and ending with the flour mixture. Scrape down the bowl after each addition. Use a whisk to break up any lumps. Fold in any additional ingredients.

6 For jumbo muffins, scoop a scant ½ cup batter into each muffin cup. For standard muffins, scoop ¼ cup batter into each muffin cup.

7 Bake standard muffins for 20 to 25 minutes and jumbo muffins for 25 to 30 minutes, until they are firm to the touch and a toothpick inserted in the middle comes out clean.

This batter is thin compared to other muffin batters, so any toppings must be added after the muffins have baked and cooled. Don't be tempted to add a nut crumble or sanding sugar; it will sink into the muffin as it bakes. (Been there! Done that!) To add a nutty crunch, dip the top of the muffin in glaze and sprinkle on toasted slivered almonds or other finely chopped nuts.

OIL-BASED MUFFIN VARIATIONS

Variation	Additional Ingredients	Suggested Toppings
Lemon–Poppy Seed	• 2 tablespoons poppy seeds • Grated zest of 1 lemon • 3 tablespoons lemon juice	• Lemon Glaze (page 291)
Tart Cherry	• 3 cups Cherry Cobbler Filling (page 286) • ¼ teaspoon almond extract	• Powdered sugar • Lemon Glaze (page 291) • Orange Glaze (page 291) • Almond Glaze (page 291)
Blueberry	• 3 cups Blueberry Cobbler Filling (page 285)	• Lemon Glaze (page 291)
Sweet Cherry	• 4 cups pitted and halved sweet cherries	• Powdered sugar • Simple Glaze (page 291) • Almond Glaze (page 291) with toasted slivered almonds
Raspberry-Rhubarb	• 2 cups raspberries • 2 cups peeled and chopped (½-inch pieces) rhubarb	• Powdered sugar • Rhubarb Frosting (page 225)

CHAPTER 2

Scones

Long before *The Great British Baking Show,* I went through my own Anglophile baking phase inspired mostly by scones, some good and a surprising number that were bad. Scones are a staple in Scotland, England, Wales, and Ireland that date back to the 1500s, but their representation in the US can be hit or miss. Sometimes, they are bland and hard; other times, they resemble extra-fluffy, overly sweet cookies. A good scone is dense, but not too dense, with just the right amount of sweetness. Too little sugar and the scone is tasteless and dry. Too much, and it covers up the essential delicate butteriness. It is the Goldilocks of pastries, and it took me a while to get it just right. Part of the problem lies in how scones are enjoyed here versus the British Isles. Across the ocean, scones are almost always eaten at the table, fresh from the oven, with each bite topped with little dollops of butter, jam, and clotted cream. Stateside, we tend to grab them with a coffee at all hours and eat them in our cars on the way to work. This recipe will satisfy both camps. It is tender and sweet enough to stand alone and a perfect base for any yummy extras you might want to add.

MIXING SCONES

Scones get their tender, flaky texture from "cutting" fat into flour. When we work solid fat, like butter or lard, into flour, the fat coats the protein in the flour, keeping some of the liquid in the recipe from reaching the protein and forming gluten. Think of gluten as elastic strands that form in dough when flour and liquid react. Gluten isn't always a baddie. Without gluten, cakes would collapse, cookies would never be delightfully chewy, and sourdough wouldn't be strong enough to trap the gas bubbles that make it rise—but developing too much gluten makes pastries tough, dense, and too heavy to fully rise when baked.

Here are three simple techniques that will have you making perfect scones in no time.

FOOD PROCESSOR

This is the fastest way to get from making scones to eating them. It is detailed step by step in the recipes that follow. You'll need a medium or large food processor. Our 2½-quart model works well. Don't be alarmed—the dough goes right up to the top of the bowl.

STAND MIXER

This is an excellent method that saves some effort if you don't have a food processor or just don't feel like getting yours out. Combine all the dry ingredients (flour, sugar, leaveners, salt, and spices) in the stand mixer bowl. Add the butter. Mix with the whip attachment at low speed until the dough is mixed enough not to fly out of the bowl. Turn the speed to medium and mix until the dough resembles a fine meal. Add any mix-ins and mix on low until evenly distributed. Add any flavorings. With the mixer running, quickly add the heavy cream. Stop the mixer before the dough comes together. Finish kneading the dough by hand on a generously floured work surface. This method can be hard on your wire whip attachment. If you plan on making a lot of scones, consider purchasing an extra.

BY HAND

The original method, which bakers have been doing for centuries. Making dough by hand is easy and fun. While it takes a bit longer, it is a good method if you want to make a bigger batch or just like getting your hands in the dough. It's also a great way to demystify the process since you literally feel the ingredients changing into dough as you mix them. For this method, combine the flour, sugar, salt, baking powder, and any spices in a medium bowl. Scatter the butter on top and toss it in the flour mixture until it is coated. Using a pastry blender, fork, or two butter knives, work the butter into the dry ingredients until it resembles a fine meal. Add any mix-ins and toss with the dough until evenly distributed. Add any flavorings. Pour the heavy cream over the dough and knead it together a couple of times in the bowl until it is evenly moist. Turn the dough out onto a generously floured work surface and knead together until smooth.

SHAPING SCONES

At the pie shop, we roll our scones 1¼ to 1½ inches thick and punch them out with a 2¾-inch square biscuit cutter. Making them all the same size and shape is efficient for us and maximizes storage space, but scones can be any shape or size. Just remember to cut back on the baking time if you make them smaller. As a quick rule of thumb, roll scones out about half as thick as the width or diameter of the biscuit cutter you choose. For example, I roll our 1-inch bite-size scones ½ inch thick. Otherwise they can become top-heavy and topple over as they rise. For the tallest, fluffiest scones, choose metal cutters with thin, sharp edges. In a pinch, a drinking glass with a smooth rim works just fine, too, though the scones won't rise quite as high. Be sure to press straight into the dough and pull straight back out. Do not twist. Twisting the cutter can seal the edges and keep the scone from fully rising or cause it to rise unevenly. Alternatively, for traditional wedge-shaped scones, roll or pat the dough into a 10-inch circle and cut into 8 equal triangles with a knife.

If you are in a hurry, scones can be baked immediately after they are shaped, but a 20- to 30-minute rest in the refrigerator will relax the gluten and chill the butter, making the scones tender and extra flaky. For straighter sides and an even rise, transfer the rested scones to the freezer for at least 20 minutes (or up to 2 weeks) and bake them off frozen. That way, the baking powder is activated before the sides of the scones thaw, forcing them to rise straight up. A dozen scones fit nicely in a gallon-size resealable freezer bag.

HISTORY

England, Ireland, Scotland, and Wales all lay claim to scones, but it is widely agreed (sometimes grudgingly) that they originated in Scotland, a descendent of the traditional bannock—a quick bread made with oats and usually cooked on a griddle. In fact, the first written record of scones was by a Scottish poet in 1513. It wasn't until the invention of commercial baking powder, some 300 years later, that scones became the lighter, oven-baked pastries we have today. The origin of the name is equally murky. The word *scone* could derive from the Dutch word *schoonbrood,* which means fine, white bread; the German word *sconbrot,* which means fine or beautiful bread; or the Scots Gaelic word *sgonn,* which means a shapeless mass or large mouthful. The least likely but most evocative theory has scones named after the Stone of Scone or Stone of Destiny, a bench-like block of red sandstone used for the coronation of Scottish kings and queens up to the 13th century and English ones thereafter. Legend says the stone "howled with joy" during the early coronations when it recognized the rightful heir to the throne.

SCONE: LIKE STONE OR SCONE: LIKE GONE?

If you are American, you probably say scone so that it rhymes with stone*; you've probably heard that the English say scone so that it rhymes with* gone. *Some do, but the posh say scone like* stone, *while others say that is a pretentious affectation. In Ireland, they say scone like* gone *in the north and like* stone *in the south. In Scotland, they say scone like* gone, *except in the village of Scone, where they say* skoon.

Top left: Add heavy cream to the food processor. Pulse just to moisten dough.
Top right: Turn crumbly dough out onto a work surface. Scatter chocolate chips or other mix-ins on top and knead together.
Bottom left: Continue kneading until dough is smooth. This may take some muscle!
Bottom right: Pound dough with a rolling pin to flatten.

Top left: Roll dough 1½ inches thick, turning occasionally to keep dough from sticking to the work surface.
Top right: Punch scones out with a square biscuit cutter.
Bottom left: Alternatively, shape dough into a 10-inch circle and cut into 8 wedges.
Bottom right: Place wedges 2 inches apart on a baking sheet.

Sweet Scone Base

This is our go-to sweet scone recipe. It bakes up delightfully crusty on the outside and manages to be both dense and tender on the inside. It is subtly sweet, the perfect medium for all kinds of additions, from the traditionally British, like dried currants and raisins, to the decidedly American, like chocolate chips. See our chart of suggested variations on page 82. The sanding sugar on top is our compromise, making it equally delightful for those of us who are likely to grab one to eat in our car with our morning coffee and those of us who will spread each bite with jam and clotted cream as we leisurely enjoy our tea. For the lightest, flakiest scones, sift the dry ingredients three times before cutting in the butter.

Ingredients

Yield: 8 or 9 (2¾-inch) square or round scones, or 8 wedge-shaped scones

4 cups	**all-purpose flour**	480g
½ cup	**granulated sugar**	100g
1½ teaspoons	**baking powder**	6g
1 teaspoon	**kosher salt**	3g
	Optional spices and/or mix-ins (see page 82)	
1 cup (2 sticks) plus 2 tablespoons	**unsalted butter, cut into ½-inch cubes and chilled**	255g
1⅓ cups	**heavy cream, plus more for brushing**	319g
	Sanding sugar, for finishing (optional)	

1. Sift the flour, granulated sugar, and baking powder three times. Transfer to the bowl of a food processor. Add the salt and any spices, if using. Add the chilled butter and process for 25 to 30 seconds, until the mixture resembles a fine meal.
2. Add the heavy cream and pulse just until it is evenly distributed. The dough should still be crumbly; it should not come together in the food processor.

3 Turn the dough out onto a lightly floured work surface. Add any mix-ins and knead together by hand until smooth. Roll the dough into a 1¼- to 1½-inch-thick square or rectangle. Punch out the scones using a 2¾-inch square or round biscuit or cookie cutter. Alternatively, for wedge-shaped scones, roll or pat the dough into a roughly 1¼- to 1½-inch-thick, 10-inch diameter circle and cut into 8 equal wedges with a knife. Dip the cutter or knife in flour between each scone.

4 Stack one rimmed baking sheet on top of another and line with parchment paper. (The double panning keeps the bottoms of the scones from overbrowning. This may not be necessary if you have an insulated or extra-heavy baking sheet.)

5 Arrange the scones at least 2 inches apart on the baking sheet. For best results, let the scones rest for 20 to 30 minutes in the fridge or freeze the scones, uncovered, for at least 20 minutes or overnight before baking.

6 Preheat the oven to 425°F.

7 Brush the tops of the scones with cream and sprinkle with sanding sugar, if using.

8 Bake for 20 to 30 minutes, rotating the sheet 180 degrees every 10 minutes, until the scones are a deep golden brown. They should feel lighter as they bake.

I like gently pulling one "test" scone slightly apart to see if it is fully baked (just be careful of those hot chocolate chips!). It should look baked but moist. It will finish cooking as it cools. The crumb should be matte. If you see any dough that still looks wet or shiny, give it a few more minutes in the oven. Don't worry; the test scone will go back together, and no one is the wiser. If not, you can always take that scone as a baker's treat!

Store wrapped, unbaked scones in the freezer for up to 2 weeks. Baked scones are best eaten the day they are made. Day-old scones can be split, toasted, and spread with butter and jam.

CHOOSING A SHAPE

Most of the scone recipes in this chapter give instructions for 2¾-inch square scones, which is how we usually make them in our shop—but scones can be any shape or size you like. Use the instructions in this base recipe for other shapes, or see "Shaping Scones" on page 76 for more ideas.

SWEET SCONE VARIATIONS

These are some of our favorite ways to use the Sweet Scone Base recipe on page 80.

Variation	Additional Ingredients	Instructions	Suggested Toppings
Chocolate Chip	• 1 cup semi-sweet chocolate chips	• Before kneading, scatter chocolate chips over the dough.	• Brush with cream, then top with sanding sugar.
Citrus-Ginger	• ½ teaspoon ground ginger • Grated zest of 2 lemons • Grated zest of 1 orange • ½ cup coarsely chopped crystallized ginger	• Add ground ginger to the food processor. Before kneading, zest lemons and orange over dough and scatter with chopped crystallized ginger.	• Brush with cream, then top with sanding sugar or citrus sanding sugar (rub a little lemon and orange zest with the sanding sugar).
Cranberry	• Grated zest of ½ orange • 1 cup halved cranberries	• Before kneading, zest orange over dough and scatter with cranberries.	• Brush with cream, then top with sanding sugar.
Cranberry-Pecan	• ⅔ cup halved cranberries • ⅓ cup toasted and chopped pecans	• Before kneading, scatter cranberries and pecans over the dough.	• Brush with cream, then top with sanding sugar or a mixture of sanding sugar and toasted pecans.
Dried Cherry	• 1 cup dried cherries	• Before kneading, scatter dried cherries over the dough.	• Brush with cream, then top with sanding sugar.
Fig, Blue Cheese & Urban Honey (full recipe page 92)	• 5 tablespoons urban honey • 1 cup crumbled blue cheese • 1 cup heavy cream (replaces 1⅓ cups in base recipe) • ¾ cup dried figs, roughly chopped	• Add honey and blue cheese to the food processor with the heavy cream. Before kneading, scatter chopped figs over the dough.	• Brush with cream, then top with sanding sugar.

Remember, for the lightest, flakiest scones, sift the dry ingredients three times before cutting in the butter.

Variation	Additional Ingredients	Instructions	Suggested Toppings
Honey-Apricot-Thyme	• 2 teaspoons finely chopped fresh thyme • 4 teaspoons honey • 1 cup roughly chopped dried apricots*	• Add thyme with the dry ingredients in the food processor. Add honey with the heavy cream. Before kneading, scatter chopped apricots over the dough.	• Brush with cream, then top with sanding sugar.
	**Roughly chopping the apricots gives you bursts of wonderful apricot flavor and keeps them from burning as the scone bakes. A few edges of apricots on the outside of the scone may get dark, but the interior will be soft and flavorful.*		
Honey-Lavender (full recipe page 95)	• 2½ teaspoons dried lavender buds • 4 teaspoons honey Honey Wash: • 1 cup honey • ⅓ cup hot water	• Pulse lavender buds with sugar in the food processor until fine before adding the other dry ingredients. Add honey with the heavy cream. • For the honey wash, mix honey and hot water until combined.	• Brush with honey wash, then top with sanding sugar.
Orange Currant	• Grated zest of 1 orange • 1 cup dried currants	• Before kneading, zest orange over dough and scatter with dried currants.	• Brush with cream, then top with sanding sugar or orange sanding sugar (rub a little orange zest with the sanding sugar).
Orange-Walnut	• ⅓ cup fresh orange juice • Grated zest of 1½ oranges • 1 cup toasted and roughly chopped walnuts	• Add orange juice with cream. Before kneading, zest oranges over dough and scatter with chopped walnuts.	• Brush with cream, then top with sanding sugar or orange sanding sugar (rub a little orange zest with the sanding sugar).
Blueberry	• Grated zest of 1 lemon • 1 cup blueberries, frozen on baking sheet overnight	• Before kneading, zest lemon over dough and scatter with frozen blueberries.	• Brush with cream, then top with sanding sugar or lemon sanding sugar (rub a little lemon zest with the sanding sugar).

Next page

SWEET SCONE VARIATIONS, *continued*

Variation	Additional Ingredients	Instructions	Suggested Toppings
Citrus–Black Raspberry (full recipe page 87)	• Grated zest of 1 lemon • Grated zest of 1 orange • 1 cup black raspberries, frozen on baking sheet overnight	• Before kneading, zest lemon and orange over dough and scatter with frozen black raspberries.	• Brush with cream, then top with sanding sugar. Drizzle with optional Sherry Vinegar Icing (page 290) when cool.
Lemon-Blueberry-Mint	• 3 tablespoons finely chopped fresh mint • 1½ cups heavy cream (replaces 1⅓ cups in base recipe) • Grated zest of 1 lemon • 1 cup blueberries, frozen on baking sheet overnight	• Add chopped mint to flour mixture in the food processor. Before kneading, zest lemon over dough and scatter with frozen blueberries.	• Brush with cream, then top with lemon-mint sanding sugar (rub a little lemon zest and mint with the sanding sugar).
Strawberry-Basil (full recipe page 100)	• ⅓ cup chopped fresh basil • 1 cup halved (or quartered if large) strawberries, frozen on baking sheet overnight	• Add chopped basil to the flour mixture in the food processor. Before kneading, scatter frozen strawberries over dough.	• Brush with cream, then top with sanding sugar.
White Chocolate–Raspberry (full recipe page 102)	• ⅓ cup white chocolate chips or roughly chopped white chocolate • ½ cup raspberries, frozen on baking sheet overnight	• Before kneading, scatter white chocolate and frozen raspberries over dough.	• Brush with cream, then top with sanding sugar. Drizzle with optional Sherry Vinegar Icing (page 290) when cool.
Maple-Pecan	• 2 tablespoons plus 2 teaspoons maple syrup • 1 cup lightly toasted and chopped pecans	• Add maple syrup with heavy cream. Before kneading, scatter pecans over dough.	• Brush with maple syrup, then top with sanding sugar or a mixture of sanding sugar and toasted pecans.
Maple-Bacon (full recipe page 97)	• 1½ teaspoons kosher salt (replaces 1 teaspoon in base recipe) • 7 strips bacon, cooked until crispy and chopped, ¼ cup bacon fat reserved • ¼ cup maple syrup	• Add bacon fat to flour mixture in the food processor with the butter. Add maple syrup with heavy cream. Before kneading, scatter chopped bacon over dough.	• Brush with maple syrup, then top with sanding sugar.

If using berries, remember to freeze them on a baking sheet the night before!

Strawberry-Basil Scones (page 100), brushed with cream and topped with sanding sugar before baking

Citrus–Black Raspberry Scones

I love everything about this recipe, from the jammy, musky black raspberries to the citrus notes, but the real star is the sherry vinegar icing. Sherry vinegar is fermented from fortified sherry, and its bright, spiced caramel flavor really comes through. It enhances the blackberries without overpowering them. Good sherry vinegar gets pricey the longer it is aged, but a basic grocery store bottle will work here.

Because scone dough is heavy and fresh berries are easily crushed, we freeze the berries individually overnight before adding them to the dough. We use this technique for all our fresh berry scones. To freeze, spread the berries in a single layer on a rimmed baking sheet or in a baking dish.

Ingredients

Yield: 8 or 9 (2¾-inch) square or round scones

4 cups	**all-purpose flour**	480g
½ cup	**granulated sugar**	100g
1½ teaspoons	**baking powder**	6g
1 teaspoon	**kosher salt**	3g
1 cup (2 sticks) plus 2 tablespoons	**unsalted butter, cut into ½-inch cubes and chilled**	255g
1⅓ cups	**heavy cream, plus more for brushing**	319g
	Grated zest of 1 lemon	
	Grated zest of 1 orange	
1 cup	**black raspberries, frozen overnight**	140g
	Sanding sugar, for finishing (optional)	
1 recipe	**Sherry Vinegar Icing (page 290), for finishing (optional)**	

Next page

CITRUS–BLACK RASPBERRY SCONES, *continued*

1 Sift the flour, granulated sugar, and baking powder three times. Transfer to the bowl of a food processor. Add the salt. Add the chilled butter and process for 25 to 30 seconds, until the mixture resembles a fine meal.

2 Add the heavy cream and pulse just until it is evenly distributed. The dough should still be crumbly; it should not come together in the food processor.

3 Turn the dough out onto a lightly floured work surface. Zest the lemon and orange over the dough and scatter with frozen black raspberries. Working quickly, knead together by hand until smooth. Roll the dough into a 1¼- to 1½-inch-thick square or rectangle.

4 Punch out the scones using a 2¾-inch square or round biscuit or cookie cutter. Dip the cutter in flour between each scone.

5 Stack one rimmed baking sheet on top of another and line with parchment paper. (The double panning keeps the bottoms of the scones from overbrowning. This may not be necessary if you have an insulated or extra-heavy baking sheet.)

6 Arrange the scones at least 2 inches apart on the baking sheet. For best results, let the scones rest for 20 to 30 minutes in the fridge or freeze the scones, uncovered, for at least 20 minutes or overnight before baking.

7 Preheat the oven to 425°F.

8 Brush the tops of the scones with cream and sprinkle with sanding sugar, if using.

9 Bake for 20 to 30 minutes, rotating the sheet 180 degrees every 10 minutes, until the scones are a deep golden brown. They should feel lighter as they bake.

10 Let cool, then drizzle with sherry vinegar icing, if using.

Store wrapped, unbaked scones in the freezer for up to 2 weeks. Baked scones are best eaten the day they are made. Day-old scones can be split, toasted, and spread with butter and jam.

Some of the frozen black raspberries will pop when you knead the dough. That's OK. The purple swirls in finished scones look fantastic!

Cranberry-Pecan Scones

Ingredients

Yield: 8 or 9 (2¾-inch) square scones

4 cups	**all-purpose flour**	480g
½ cup	**granulated sugar**	100g
1½ teaspoons	**baking powder**	6g
1 teaspoon	**kosher salt**	3g
1 cup (2 sticks) plus 2 tablespoons	**unsalted butter, cut into ½-inch cubes and chilled**	255g
1⅓ cups	**heavy cream, plus more for brushing**	319g
⅔ cup	**fresh cranberries, halved**	67g
½ cup	**toasted and roughly chopped pecans**	60g
	Sanding sugar, for finishing (optional)	

1 Sift the flour, granulated sugar, and baking powder three times. Transfer to the bowl of a food processor. Add the salt and chilled butter and process for 25 to 30 seconds, until the mixture resembles a fine meal.

2 Add the heavy cream and pulse just until it is evenly distributed. The dough should still be crumbly; it should not come together in the food processor.

3 Turn the dough out onto a lightly floured work surface. Scatter the cranberries and pecans over the dough and knead together by hand until smooth. Roll the dough into a 1¼- to 1½-inch-thick square or rectangle.

4 Punch out the scones using a 2¾-inch square biscuit or cookie cutter. Dip the cutter in flour between each scone.

5 Stack one rimmed baking sheet on top of another and line with parchment paper. (The double panning keeps the bottoms of the scones from overbrowning. This may not be necessary if you have an insulated or extra-heavy baking sheet.)

Next page

CRANBERRY-PECAN SCONES, *continued*

6 Arrange the scones at least 2 inches apart on the baking sheet. For best results, let the scones rest for 20 to 30 minutes in the fridge or freeze the scones, uncovered, for at least 20 minutes or overnight before baking.

7 Preheat the oven to 425°F.

8 Brush the tops of the scones with cream and sprinkle with sanding sugar, if using.

9 Bake for 20 to 30 minutes, rotating the sheet 180 degrees every 10 minutes, until the scones are a deep golden brown. They should feel lighter as they bake.

Store wrapped, unbaked scones in the freezer for up to 2 weeks. Baked scones are best eaten the day they are made. Day-old scones can be split, toasted, and spread with butter and jam.

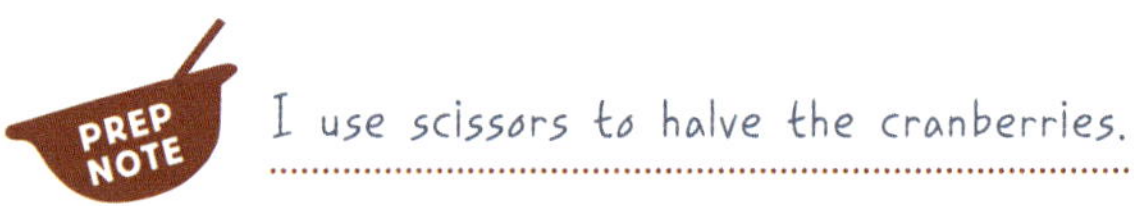

I use scissors to halve the cranberries.

Fig, Blue Cheese & Urban Honey Scones

If you can, seek out urban honey for this recipe, which balances sweet and savory flavors. It has a unique, subtle taste, which includes hints of mint, menthol, and salt. I reach for urban honey anytime I want a complex honey flavor that's not overly sweet.

Ingredients

Yield: 8 or 9 (2¾-inch) square scones

4 cups	**all-purpose flour**	480g
1 tablespoon plus 2 teaspoons	**granulated sugar**	18g
1 tablespoon	**baking powder**	12g
1¼ teaspoons	**kosher salt**	3.75g
1¼ cups (2½ sticks)	**unsalted butter, cut into ½-inch cubes and chilled**	283g
1 cup	**crumbled blue cheese**	113g
5 tablespoons	**urban honey**	105g
1 cup	**heavy cream**	240g
¾ cup	**dried figs, roughly chopped**	128g
	Sanding sugar, for finishing (optional)	

1. Sift the flour, granulated sugar, and baking powder three times. Transfer to the bowl of a food processor. Add the salt and chilled butter and process for 25 to 30 seconds, until the mixture resembles a fine meal.
2. Add the blue cheese, honey, and heavy cream and pulse just until it is evenly distributed. The dough should still be crumbly; it should not come together in the food processor.
3. Turn the dough out onto a lightly floured work surface. Scatter the chopped figs over the dough and knead together by hand until smooth. Roll the dough into a ½-inch-thick square or rectangle.
4. Punch out the scones using a 2¾-inch square biscuit or cookie cutter. Dip the cutter in flour between each scone.

5 Stack one rimmed baking sheet on top of another and line with parchment paper. (The double panning keeps the bottoms of the scones from overbrowning. This may not be necessary if you have an insulated or extra-heavy baking sheet.)

6 Arrange the scones at least 2 inches apart on the baking sheet. For best results, let the scones rest for 20 to 30 minutes in the fridge or freeze the scones, uncovered, for at least 20 minutes or overnight before baking.

7 Preheat the oven to 425°F.

8 Brush the tops of the scones with cream and sprinkle with sanding sugar, if using.

9 Bake for 15 to 20 minutes, rotating the sheet 180 degrees every 10 minutes, until the scones are a deep golden brown. They should feel lighter as they bake.

Store wrapped, unbaked scones in the freezer for up to 2 weeks. Baked scones are best eaten the day they are made. Day-old scones can be split, toasted, and spread with butter and jam.

URBAN BEE

When you think of beekeeping, you picture sunny fields of wildflowers and dusty country roads, but honeybees also thrive in cities. They may even be healthier and more productive than their country cousins, thanks to biodiversity and the absence of farm chemicals. In the past decade, New York, Milwaukee, and Los Angeles all lifted century-old bans on urban hives, welcoming an influx of buzzy new city dwellers. Thanks to a 2014 Obama-era initiative, Washington, DC, is now home to some two hundred million bees in colonies across the city, including one in a "secure compound" at the US State Department. In Chicago, the Department of Aviation, taking a macro approach to their job, hosts seventy-five hives in a grassy field just off a busy runway at O'Hare Airport. In 2015, they took home a blue ribbon for their honey at the Illinois State Fair.

What does urban honey taste like?

Urban bees collect nectar from an impressive variety of plants, from the flowers in your garden to weeds growing in pavement cracks to trees planted in public spaces. All this gives urban honey a complex flavor that varies from city to city and neighborhood to neighborhood. Most often, you taste notes of menthol and mint, offsetting honey's cloying sweetness. This comes from linden trees. Shady, pretty linden trees grow unbothered by pollution, wind, drought, and other harsh urban conditions. They are popular with city planners—and with the honeybees that flock to their fragrant pale yellow flowers in the spring.

Honey-Lavender Scones

This scone has a devoted following, especially among our farmers' market customers. We know we're gonna hear about it if they're not in the pastry case on Saturday mornings. It's popular with grown-ups, kids, and at least one rambunctious golden retriever named Sammy. Sammy is the unofficial mayor of the farmers' market. While his human works at a farmstand, Sammy greets marketgoers, checks on all the vendors, and ensures the pigeons and seagulls behave themselves. One Saturday, to everyone's astonishment, Sammy grabbed a bag containing a honey-lavender scone from a customer's hand and took off running. We were alerted when Sammy's sheepish owner came by to replace it. While we don't know how Sammy developed a taste for scones (we suspect someone was literally feeding him under the table), the delightful aroma of honey-lavender scones baking does fill the kitchen. Whip up a batch and see who comes running.

Ingredients

Yield: 8 or 9 (2¾-inch) square scones

2½ teaspoons	**dried lavender buds**	2.5g
½ cup	**granulated sugar**	100g
4 cups	**all-purpose flour**	480g
1½ teaspoons	**baking powder**	6g
1 teaspoon	**kosher salt**	3g
1 cup (2 sticks) plus 2 tablespoons	**unsalted butter, cut into ½-inch cubes and chilled**	255g
⅓ cup plus 4 teaspoons	**honey, divided**	127g
1⅓ cups	**heavy cream, plus more for brushing**	319g
⅓ cup	**hot water**	80g
	Sanding sugar, for finishing (optional)	

Next page

HONEY-LAVENDER SCONES, *continued*

1. Pulse the lavender buds with the granulated sugar in a food processor until fine. The mixture may resemble powdered sugar when you are done—that's OK.
2. Sift the flour and baking powder three times. Transfer to the bowl of the food processor with the lavender sugar. Add the salt and chilled butter and process for 25 to 30 seconds, until the mixture resembles a fine meal.
3. Add 4 teaspoons of the honey and the heavy cream and pulse just until it is evenly distributed. The dough should still be crumbly; it should not come together in the food processor.
4. Turn the dough out onto a lightly floured work surface and knead together by hand until smooth. Roll the dough into a 1¼- to 1½-inch-thick square or rectangle.
5. Punch out the scones using a 2¾-inch square biscuit or cookie cutter. Dip the cutter in flour between each scone.
6. Stack one rimmed baking sheet on top of another and line with parchment paper. (The double panning keeps the bottoms of the scones from overbrowning. This may not be necessary if you have an insulated or extra-heavy baking sheet.)
7. Arrange the scones at least 2 inches apart on the baking sheet. For best results, let the scones rest for 20 to 30 minutes in the fridge or freeze the scones, uncovered, for at least 20 minutes or overnight before baking.
8. Preheat the oven to 425°F.
9. In a small bowl, mix the hot water and remaining ⅓ cup honey until well combined. Brush the tops of the scones with the honey mixture and sprinkle with sanding sugar, if using.
10. Bake for 20 to 30 minutes, rotating the sheet 180 degrees every 10 minutes, until the scones are a deep golden brown. They should feel lighter as they bake.

Store wrapped, unbaked scones in the freezer for up to 2 weeks. Baked scones are best eaten the day they are made. Day-old scones can be split, toasted, and spread with butter and jam.

Because of the honey on top, these scones brown faster and bake darker than others. This is why we water down the honey.

Maple-Bacon Scones

As anyone who has ever surreptitiously dipped their bacon into the maple syrup on their pancakes knows, maple and bacon taste great together. The bacon fat in the recipe makes these scones extra tender. Be sure to cook the bacon until it just starts to crisp up. Any less and the bacon turns mushy in the dough, much more and it ends up tasting burnt once the scones cook. If you don't have enough bacon fat for the recipe after you cook the bacon, make up the difference in butter.

Ingredients

Yield: 8 or 9 (2¾-inch) square or round scones

7 strips	**bacon**	~210g
4 cups	**all-purpose flour**	480g
½ cup	**granulated sugar**	100g
1½ teaspoons	**baking powder**	6g
1½ teaspoons	**kosher salt**	4.5g
1 cup (2 sticks) plus 2 tablespoons	**unsalted butter, cut into ½-inch cubes and chilled**	255g
1⅓ cups	**heavy cream**	319g
¼ cup	**maple syrup, plus more for brushing**	85g
	Sanding sugar, for finishing (optional)	

1 Cook the bacon until it is golden brown and the edges are crispy. Reserve ¼ cup of the bacon fat. When the bacon is cool, pat it dry with paper towels and roughly chop. Set aside.

2 Sift the flour, sugar, and baking powder three times. Transfer to the bowl of a medium food processor. Add the salt, chilled butter, and reserved bacon fat and process for 25 to 30 seconds, until the mixture resembles a fine meal.

Next page

MAPLE-BACON SCONES, *continued*

3 Add the heavy cream and maple syrup and pulse just until it is evenly distributed. The dough should still be crumbly; it should not come together in the food processor.

4 Turn the dough out onto a lightly floured work surface and knead together by hand until smooth. Knead the bacon pieces into the dough. Roll the dough into a 1¼- to 1½-inch-thick square or rectangle.

5 Punch out the scones using a 2¾-inch square or round biscuit or cookie cutter. Dip the cutter in flour between each scone.

6 Stack one rimmed baking sheet on top of another and line with parchment paper. (The double panning keeps the bottoms of the scones from overbrowning. This may not be necessary if you have an insulated or extra-heavy baking sheet.)

7 Arrange the scones at least 2 inches apart on the baking sheet. For best results, let the scones rest for 20 to 30 minutes in the fridge or freeze the scones, uncovered, for at least 20 minutes or overnight before baking.

8 Preheat the oven to 425°F.

9 Brush the tops of the scones with maple syrup and sprinkle with sanding sugar, if using.

10 Bake for 20 to 30 minutes, rotating the sheet 180 degrees every 10 minutes, until the scones are a deep golden brown. They should feel lighter as they bake.

Store wrapped, unbaked scones in the freezer for up to 2 weeks. Baked scones are best eaten the day they are made. Day-old scones can be split, toasted, and spread with butter and jam.

Strawberry-Basil Scones

Ingredients

Yield: 8 or 9 (2¾-inch) square scones, or 8 wedge-shaped scones

4 cups	**all-purpose flour**	480g
½ cup	**granulated sugar**	100g
1½ teaspoons	**baking powder**	6g
1 teaspoon	**kosher salt**	3g
⅓ cup	**chopped fresh basil**	8g
1 cup (2 sticks) plus 2 tablespoons	**unsalted butter, cut into ½-inch cubes and chilled**	255g
1⅓ cups	**heavy cream, plus more for brushing**	319g
1 cup	**halved (or quartered if large) strawberries, frozen overnight**	140g
	Sanding sugar, for finishing (optional)	

1. Sift the flour, granulated sugar, and baking powder three times. Transfer to the bowl of a food processor. Add the salt, basil, and chilled butter and process for 25 to 30 seconds, until the mixture resembles a fine meal.
2. Add the heavy cream and pulse just until it is evenly distributed. The dough should still be crumbly; it should not come together in the food processor.
3. Turn the dough out onto a lightly floured work surface. Scatter the frozen strawberries over the dough. Working quickly, knead together by hand until smooth. Roll the dough into a 1¼- to 1½-inch-thick square or rectangle. (Or, for wedge-shaped scones, follow rolling and cutting instructions on page 81.)
4. Punch out the scones using a 2¾-inch square biscuit or cookie cutter. Dip the cutter in flour between each scone.
5. Stack one rimmed baking sheet on top of another and line with parchment paper. (The double panning keeps the bottoms of the scones from overbrowning. This may not be necessary if you have an insulated or extra-heavy baking sheet.)

6 Arrange the scones at least 2 inches apart on the baking sheet. For best results, let the scones rest for 20 to 30 minutes in the fridge or freeze the scones, uncovered, for at least 20 minutes or overnight before baking.

7 Preheat the oven to 425°F.

8 Brush the tops of the scones with cream and sprinkle with sanding sugar, if using.

9 Bake for 20 to 30 minutes, rotating the sheet 180 degrees every 10 minutes, until the scones are a deep golden brown. They should feel lighter as they bake.

Store wrapped, unbaked scones in the freezer for up to 2 weeks. Baked scones are best eaten the day they are made. Day-old scones can be split, toasted, and spread with butter and jam.

White Chocolate–Raspberry Scones

Ingredients

Yield: 8 or 9 (2¾-inch) square scones

4 cups	**all-purpose flour**	480g
½ cup	**granulated sugar**	100g
1½ teaspoons	**baking powder**	6g
1 teaspoon	**kosher salt**	3g
1 cup (2 sticks) plus 2 tablespoons	**unsalted butter, cut into ½-inch cubes and chilled**	255g
1⅓ cups	**heavy cream, plus more for brushing**	319g
⅓ cup	**white chocolate chips or chopped white chocolate**	57g
½ cup	**raspberries, frozen overnight**	62g
	Sanding sugar, for finishing (optional)	
1 recipe	**Sherry Vinegar Icing (page 290), for finishing (optional)**	

1 Sift the flour, granulated sugar, and baking powder three times. Transfer to the bowl of a food processor. Add the salt and chilled butter and process for 25 to 30 seconds, until the mixture resembles a fine meal.

2 Add the heavy cream and pulse just until it is evenly distributed. The dough should still be crumbly; it should not come together in the food processor.

3 Turn the dough out onto a lightly floured work surface. Scatter the white chocolate and frozen raspberries over the dough. Working quickly, knead together by hand until smooth. Roll the dough into a 1¼- to 1½-inch-thick square or rectangle.

4 Punch out the scones using a 2¾-inch square biscuit or cookie cutter. Dip the cutter in flour between each scone.

5 Stack one rimmed baking sheet on top of another and line with parchment paper. (The double panning keeps the bottoms of the scones from overbrowning. This may not be necessary if you have an insulated or extra-heavy baking sheet.)

6 Arrange the scones at least 2 inches apart on the baking sheet. For best results, let the scones rest for 20 to 30 minutes in the fridge or freeze the scones, uncovered, for at least 20 minutes or overnight before baking.

7 Preheat the oven to 425°F.

8 Brush the tops of the scones with cream and sprinkle with sanding sugar, if using.

9 Bake for 20 to 30 minutes, rotating the sheet 180 degrees every 10 minutes, until the scones are a deep golden brown. They should feel lighter as they bake.

10 Let cool, then drizzle with sherry vinegar icing, if using.

Store wrapped, unbaked scones in the freezer for up to 2 weeks. Baked scones are best eaten the day they are made. Day-old scones can be split, toasted, and spread with butter and jam.

Chocolate-Ginger Scones

Chocolate and ginger, especially candied ginger, is a delightful combination—somehow exotic and comforting at the same time. Baking chocolate scones is tricky since you can't rely on color to tell when they are done. The pull-apart method is more important here, so be sure to have a cup of coffee or tea handy in case you end up with a "test" scone.

Ingredients

Yield: 9 or 10 (2 ¾-inch) square scones

5 cups	**all-purpose flour**	600g
2 cups	**Dutch-processed cocoa powder**	170g
1 cup	**granulated sugar**	200g
3 tablespoons	**baking powder**	36g
2 teaspoons	**ground ginger, plus more for ginger sugar (optional)**	4g
2 tablespoons	**kosher salt**	18g
1¾ cups (3 ½ sticks)	**unsalted butter, cut into ½-inch cubes and chilled**	396g
1 cup	**heavy cream, plus more for brushing**	240g
1 cup	**roughly chopped crystallized ginger**	160g
	Sanding sugar, for finishing (optional)	

1. Sift the flour, cocoa powder, granulated sugar, baking powder, and ground ginger three times. Transfer to the bowl of a food processor. Add the salt and chilled butter and process for 25 to 30 seconds, until the mixture resembles a fine meal.
2. Add the heavy cream and pulse just until it is evenly distributed. The dough should still be crumbly; it should not come together in the food processor.

Next page

CHOCOLATE-GINGER SCONES, *continued*

3 Turn the dough out onto a lightly floured work surface (see prep note). Scatter the chopped ginger over the dough and knead together by hand until smooth. Roll the dough into a 1¼- to 1½-inch-thick square or rectangle.

4 Punch out the scones using a 2¾-inch square biscuit or cookie cutter. Dip the cutter in flour between each scone.

5 Stack one rimmed baking sheet on top of another and line with parchment paper. (The double panning keeps the bottoms of the scones from overbrowning. This may not be necessary if you have an insulated or extra-heavy baking sheet.)

6 Arrange the scones at least 2 inches apart on the baking sheet. For best results, let the scones rest for 20 to 30 minutes in the fridge or freeze the scones, uncovered, for at least 20 minutes or overnight before baking.

7 Preheat the oven to 425°F.

8 To make the optional ginger sugar, in a small bowl, combine 1 part sanding sugar with 1 part ground ginger and mix.

9 Brush the tops of the scones with cream and sprinkle with sanding sugar or ginger sugar, if using.

10 Bake the scones for 20 to 30 minutes, rotating the sheet 180 degrees every 10 minutes. Baked scones should feel firm and light and sound hollow when gently tapped on the bottom. If you are still unsure, use the pull-apart method (see page 81) or an instant-read thermometer. Scones are ready when they have reached an internal temperature of 200 to 205°F.

Store wrapped, unbaked scones in the freezer for up to 2 weeks. Baked scones are best eaten the day they are made. Day-old scones can be split, toasted, and spread with butter and jam.

Using flour alone for rolling can leave white streaks on the dark scones. I use a mixture that is equal parts cocoa powder and flour.

Pumpkin Scones

Everyone is excited when the first batch of pumpkin scones comes out of the oven in the fall. It doesn't hurt that you can smell the warm spices baking all over the shop and down the street. (It is a happy design quirk at both shops that the exhaust fans vent over the sidewalk.)

Ingredients

Yield: 9 or 10 (2¾-inch) square scones, or 8 wedge-shaped scones

4⅓ cups	**all-purpose flour**	520g
⅔ cup	**packed dark brown sugar**	142g
2 teaspoons	**baking powder**	8g
1 teaspoon	**ground ginger**	2g
1 teaspoon	**ground cinnamon**	2.6g
½ teaspoon	**baking soda**	2g
½ teaspoon	**kosher salt**	1.5g
1 cup (2 sticks)	**unsalted butter, cut into ½-inch cubes and chilled**	227g
1 cup	**canned pumpkin puree**	245g
⅔ cup	**buttermilk, plus more for brushing**	151g
2 teaspoons	**vanilla paste**	10g
1 cup	**sanding sugar**	200g
2 tablespoons	**pumpkin pie spice**	14g

1. Sift the flour, brown sugar, baking powder, ginger, cinnamon, and baking soda three times. Transfer to the bowl of a food processor. Add the salt and chilled butter and process for 25 to 30 seconds, until the mixture resembles a fine meal.
2. Add the pumpkin puree, buttermilk, and vanilla paste and pulse just until it is evenly distributed. The dough should still be crumbly; it should not come together in the food processor.
3. Turn the dough out onto a lightly floured work surface and knead together by hand until smooth. Roll the dough into a 1¼- to 1½-inch-thick square or rectangle. (Or, for wedge-shaped scones, follow rolling and cutting instructions on page 81.)

Next page

PUMPKIN SCONES, *continued*

4 Punch out the scones using a 2¾-inch square biscuit or cookie cutter. Dip the cutter in flour between each scone.

5 Stack one rimmed baking sheet on top of another and line with parchment paper. (The double panning keeps the bottoms of the scones from overbrowning. This may not be necessary if you have an insulated or extra-heavy baking sheet.)

6 Arrange the scones at least 2 inches apart on the baking sheet. For best results, let the scones rest for 20 to 30 minutes in the fridge or freeze the scones, uncovered, for at least 20 minutes or overnight before baking.

7 Preheat the oven to 425°F.

8 In a small bowl, mix the sanding sugar and pumpkin pie spice, rubbing it together with your fingertips until the spice is evenly distributed.

9 Brush the tops of the scones with buttermilk and sprinkle with the pumpkin spice sanding sugar.

10 Bake for 20 to 30 minutes, rotating the sheet 180 degrees every 10 minutes, until the bottoms of the scones start to brown. Baked scones should feel firm and light and sound hollow when gently tapped on the bottom. Use the pull-apart method (see page 81) or an instant-read thermometer if you are still unsure. Scones are ready when they have an internal temperature of 200 to 205°F.

Store wrapped, unbaked scones in the freezer for up to 2 weeks. Baked scones are best eaten the day they are made. Day-old scones can be split, toasted, and spread with butter and jam.

Sweet Potato Scones

This sweet potato variation of our Pumpkin Scones (page 107) requires a bit more work but is well worth the extra effort. If you are lucky enough to find purple sweet potatoes, give them a try. They taste like the familiar orange variety with jammy, winey, almost Juicy Fruit notes thrown in; plus, the finished purple-hued scones look amazing!

Ingredients

Yield: 9 or 10 (2 ¾-inch) square scones

2	**medium sweet potatoes, well scrubbed**	300–400g total
4 ⅓ cups	**all-purpose flour**	520g
⅔ cup	**packed dark brown sugar**	142g
¼ teaspoon	**freshly ground black pepper**	0.6g
2 teaspoons	**baking powder**	8g
1 teaspoon	**ground cinnamon**	2.6g
½ teaspoon	**baking soda**	2g
½ teaspoon	**kosher salt**	1.5g
	Grated zest of ½ orange	
1 cup (2 sticks)	**unsalted butter, cut into ½-inch cubes and chilled**	227g
⅔ cup	**buttermilk, plus more for brushing**	151g
2 teaspoons	**vanilla paste**	10g
	Sanding sugar, for finishing (optional)	
1 recipe	**Simple Glaze (page 291), for finishing (optional)**	
	Tajín, for finishing (optional)	

1 Preheat the oven to 400°F.

2 Prick the sweet potatoes all over with a fork or small knife. Place on a rimmed baking sheet and bake for 45 to 60 minutes, until the potatoes are very soft. (For purple sweet potatoes, preheat the oven to 350°F and bake for 90 to 120 minutes.) Set aside until cool enough to handle, but no longer than 2 hours (see "Baking and Storing Potatoes" on page 68).

3 Cut the sweet potatoes in half and scoop the flesh into the bowl of a food processor, stand mixer, food mill, or potato ricer. Process or mash until smooth. (You can also mash the potatoes by hand.) If desired, press the sweet potato puree through a fine-mesh sieve for a smoother texture.

4 Sift the flour, brown sugar, black pepper, baking powder, cinnamon, and baking soda three times. (If the black pepper is too coarse to pass through a sifter, add it directly to the bowl of the food processor.) Transfer the flour mixture to the bowl of a food processor. Add the salt and zest the orange over the flour mixture. Add the chilled butter and process for 25 to 30 seconds, until the mixture resembles a fine meal.

5 Add 1 cup of the sweet potato puree (reserve the rest in the refrigerator for another use), the buttermilk, and vanilla paste and pulse just until it is evenly distributed. The dough should still be crumbly; it should not come together in the food processor.

6 Turn the dough out onto a lightly floured work surface and knead together by hand until smooth. Roll the dough into a 1¼- to 1½-inch-thick square or rectangle.

7 Punch out the scones using a 2¾-inch square biscuit or cookie cutter. Dip the cutter in flour between each scone.

8 Stack one rimmed baking sheet on top of another and line with parchment paper. (The double panning keeps the bottoms of the scones from overbrowning. This may not be necessary if you have an insulated or extra-heavy baking sheet.)

9 Arrange the scones at least 2 inches apart on the baking sheet. For best results, let the scones rest for 20 to 30 minutes in the fridge or freeze the scones, uncovered, for at least 20 minutes or overnight before baking.

10 Preheat the oven to 450°F.

11 Brush the tops of the scones with buttermilk and sprinkle with sanding sugar, if using.

12 Bake for 20 to 30 minutes, rotating the sheet 180 degrees every 10 minutes, until the bottoms of the scones start to brown. Baked scones should feel firm and light and sound hollow when gently tapped on the bottom. Use the pull-apart method (see page 81) or an instant-read thermometer if you are still unsure. Scones are ready when they have an internal temperature of 200 to 205°F.

13 Let cool, then drizzle with simple glaze, if using. For purple sweet potato scones, drizzle with simple glaze and, once it is set, dust with Tajín, shaking off any excess.

Store wrapped, unbaked scones in the freezer for up to 2 weeks. Baked scones are best eaten the day they are made. Day-old scones can be split, toasted, and spread with butter and jam.

Buckwheat-Date Scones

If you are not familiar with buckwheat flour, you're in for a treat. It has a malty, earthy, molasses flavor with a hops-like finish that adds depth to all kinds of baked goods. It is a traditional ingredient in French crepes, Japanese noodles, and American pancakes. Once you have some on hand, you'll find yourself adding it to all kinds of recipes. It pairs well with other earthy flavors like figs, raisins, molasses, and dark honey (especially buckwheat honey). I also like to use it as a foil in pastries that might otherwise be too cloyingly sweet, like jam bars or filled cookies. Unlike traditional flour, it is not a grain at all. It is the ground-up starchy seeds of a lovely plant with heart-shaped leaves and clusters of white-and-pink flowers. It is more closely related to sorrel and rhubarb than wheat and is entirely gluten-free. For that reason, it won't replace all the traditional flour in a recipe, but you can safely swap out 20 to 30 percent without making any other changes.

Ingredients

Yield: 8 or 9 (2¾-inch) square scones

2⅓ cups	**all-purpose flour**	280g
1⅓ cups	**buckwheat flour**	160g
½ cup	**granulated sugar**	100g
1½ teaspoons	**baking powder**	6g
1 teaspoon	**kosher salt**	3g
1 cup (2 sticks) plus 2 tablespoons	**unsalted butter, cut into ½-inch cubes and chilled**	255g
1⅓ cups	**heavy cream, plus more for brushing**	319g
1⅓ cups	**roughly chopped pitted dates**	200g
	Sanding sugar, for finishing (optional)	
1 recipe	**Sherry Vinegar Icing (page 290), for finishing (optional)**	

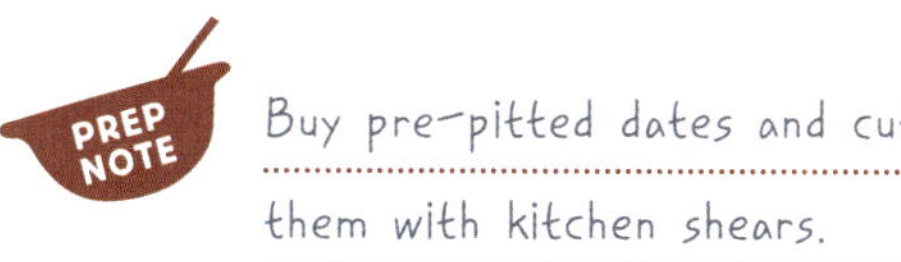

Buy pre-pitted dates and cut them with kitchen shears.

Next page

BUCKWHEAT-DATE SCONES, *continued*

1 Sift the all-purpose flour, buckwheat flour, granulated sugar, and baking powder three times. Transfer to the bowl of a food processor. Add the salt and chilled butter and process for 25 to 30 seconds until the mixture resembles a fine meal.

2 Add the heavy cream and pulse just until it is evenly distributed. The dough should still be crumbly; it should not come together in the food processor.

3 Turn the dough out onto a lightly floured work surface. Scatter the chopped dates over the dough and knead together by hand until smooth.

4 Roll the dough into a 1¼- to 1½-inch-thick square or rectangle.

5 Punch out the scones using a 2¾-inch square biscuit or cookie cutter. Dip the cutter in flour between each scone.

6 Stack one rimmed baking sheet on top of another and line with parchment paper. (The double panning keeps the bottoms of the scones from overbrowning. This may not be necessary if you have an insulated or extra-heavy baking sheet.)

7 Arrange the scones at least 2 inches apart on the baking sheet. For best results, let the scones rest for 20 to 30 minutes in the fridge or freeze the scones, uncovered, for at least 20 minutes or overnight before baking.

8 Preheat the oven to 425°F.

9 Brush the tops of the scones with cream and sprinkle with sanding sugar, if using.

10 Bake for 20 to 30 minutes, rotating the sheet 180 degrees every 10 minutes, until the scones are a deep golden brown. They should feel lighter as they bake.

11 Let cool, then drizzle with sherry vinegar icing, if using.

Store wrapped, unbaked scones in the freezer for up to 2 weeks. Baked scones are best eaten the day they are baked, preferably warm from the oven (unless you are finishing them with icing). Day-old scones can be split, toasted, and spread with butter, cream cheese, or Apple Butter (page 274).

***Whole-grain flours, like whole wheat, rye, and buckwheat,** contain more oil than all-purpose flour and can turn rancid fairly quickly when exposed to heat and light. Store whole-grain flours in an airtight container in a cool, dry, dark space like a pantry for up to 2 months. If you are not going to use them in that time, you can store them in the freezer for up to 1 year. If the flour smells rancid—like burnt silicone or pencil erasers—toss it out and replace it.*

White Chocolate & Orange Rye Scones

Rye is another great alternative flour to keep on hand. When you think of rye flavor, you probably imagine the strong citrusy-licorice flavor of the caraway seeds you find in most rye bread. On its own, rye is much more subtle. It is slightly sour and nutty, with hints of toasted baking spices and coriander. It pairs especially well with chocolate and citrus. If you want to experiment, you can generally substitute rye flour 1 to 1 by weight for all-purpose flour in recipes with chemical leaveners like baking powder and baking soda. It does contain gluten, but it is less stretchy than the gluten in wheat flour, so it can be tricky when used in yeast-raised pastries.

Ingredients

Yield: 8 or 9 (2¾-inch) square scones

2 ⅓ cups	**all-purpose flour**	280g
1⅓ cups	**rye flour**	160g
½ cup	**granulated sugar**	100g
1½ teaspoons	**baking powder**	6g
1 teaspoon	**kosher salt**	3g
1 cup (2 sticks) plus 2 tablespoons	**unsalted butter, cut into ½-inch cubes and chilled**	255g
1⅓ cups	**heavy cream, plus more for brushing**	319g
½ cup	**chopped Candied Orange Peel (page 296)**	85g
1 cup	**white chocolate chips or chopped white chocolate**	170g
	Sanding sugar, for finishing (optional)	

1 Sift the all-purpose flour, rye flour, granulated sugar, and baking powder three times. Transfer to the bowl of a food processor. Add the salt and chilled butter and process for 25 to 30 seconds, until the mixture resembles a fine meal.

Next page

WHITE CHOCOLATE & ORANGE RYE SCONES, *continued*

2 Add the heavy cream and candied orange peel and pulse until evenly distributed. The dough should still be crumbly; it should not come together in the food processor.

3 Turn the dough out onto a lightly floured work surface. Scatter the white chocolate chips over the dough and knead the dough together by hand until smooth. Roll the dough into a 1¼- to 1½-inch-thick square or rectangle.

4 Punch out the scones using a 2¾-inch square biscuit or cookie cutter. Dip the cutter in flour between each scone.

5 Stack one rimmed baking sheet on top of another and line with parchment paper. (The double panning keeps the bottoms of the scones from overbrowning. This may not be necessary if you have an insulated or extra-heavy baking sheet.)

6 Arrange the scones at least 2 inches apart on the baking sheet. For best results, let the scones rest for 20 to 30 minutes in the fridge or freeze the scones, uncovered, for at least 20 minutes or overnight before baking.

7 Preheat the oven to 425°F.

8 Brush the tops of scones with cream and sprinkle with sanding sugar, if using.

9 Bake for 20 to 30 minutes, rotating the sheet 180 degrees every 10 minutes, until the scones are a deep golden brown. They should feel lighter as they bake.

Store wrapped, unbaked scones in the freezer for up to 2 weeks. Baked scones are best eaten the day they are made. Day-old scones can be split, toasted, and spread with butter and jam.

IT'S FOUR O'CLOCK SOMEWHERE

In 1840, a lady-in-waiting got hangry, and the tradition of afternoon tea was born. Anna Russell, the Duchess of Bedford, complained of a "sinking feeling" in the hours between the traditional midday lunch and her household's fashionably late 8 p.m. dinner. She started requesting that a tray of tea, bread, butter, cake, and scones be brought to her room at precisely 4 p.m. every afternoon. She found this snack so delightful that she soon asked her friends to join her. One of her friends was Queen Victoria, who quickly gave the practice her royal endorsement. Why not treat yourself like royalty? Whip up a batch of scones and invite your friends over. Any time of day will do. After all, it's four o'clock somewhere.

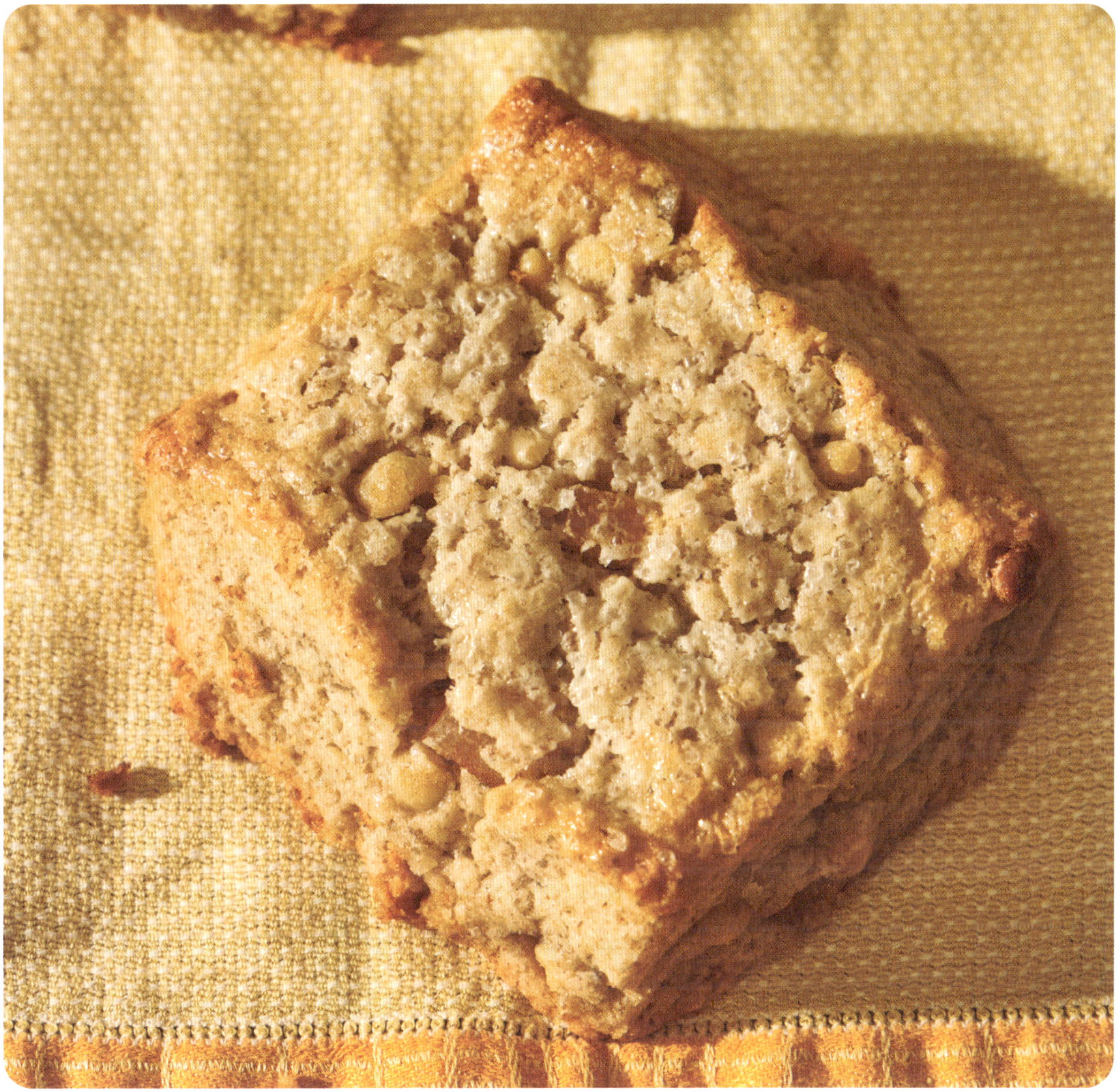

PREP NOTE

Candying orange peel is time-consuming but quite simple, and the result is worlds away from the gummy, bitter candied citron you buy at the grocery store. Our recipe makes more than you need for these scones, but smaller batches are harder to control and tend to overcaramelize quickly.

Cheddar-Jalapeño Scones

This scone was an instant hit at the shop, where our biggest production problem was keeping the pie slingers from eating them all. Even if you don't like spicy food, don't be afraid of the peppers. Sautéing the jalapeños in butter adds a mellow flavor without much heat. I like to cut these scones smaller and treat them like gougères (small French cheese puffs) or cheese straws eaten in one or two bites as an hors d'oeuvre. Or you can cut these into hearty wedges to pair with black bean soup or chicken chili.

Ingredients

Yield: 48 (1¾-inch) bite-size round scones, or 8 wedge-shaped scones

1¼ cups (2½ sticks)	**unsalted butter, divided**	284g
2	**large jalapeño peppers, seeded, ribs removed, and finely chopped**	60g
2 teaspoons	**kosher salt, plus more for seasoning**	6g
4 cups	**all-purpose flour**	480g
1 tablespoon	**sugar**	12g
1 tablespoon	**baking powder**	12g
1 tablespoon	**ground mustard**	6g
1 teaspoon	**freshly ground black pepper, plus more for seasoning**	2g
2 cups	**shredded or grated sharp or extra-sharp cheddar cheese**	226g
1 cup	**heavy cream**	240g
1	**large egg, lightly beaten**	50g

1 Cut 1 cup of the butter into ½-inch cubes and keep refrigerated until ready to use.

2 Melt the remaining ¼ cup butter in a small sauté pan over medium-low heat. Add the chopped jalapeños and sprinkle generously with salt. Turn the heat down to low and cook, stirring frequently, until the peppers soften, about 3 minutes. They should not brown. Set aside to cool.

Next page

CHEDDAR-JALAPEÑO SCONES, *continued*

3 Sift the flour, sugar, baking powder, mustard, and black pepper three times. (If the black pepper is too coarse to pass through a sifter, add it directly to the bowl of the food processor.) Transfer the flour mixture to the bowl of a food processor. Add the salt and chilled butter and process for 25 to 30 seconds, until the mixture resembles a fine meal.

4 Add the cheddar cheese, sautéed jalapeños, and heavy cream and pulse just until it is evenly distributed. The dough should still be crumbly; it should not come together in the food processor.

5 Turn the dough out onto a lightly floured work surface and knead together by hand until smooth. Roll the dough into a ½-inch-thick rectangle. (Or, for wedge-shaped scones, follow rolling and cutting instructions on page 81.)

6 Punch out the scones using a 1¾-inch round fluted biscuit or cookie cutter. Dip the cutter in flour between each scone.

7 Stack one rimmed baking sheet on top of another and line with parchment paper. (The double panning keeps the bottoms of the scones from overbrowning. This may not be necessary if you have an insulated or extra-heavy baking sheet.)

8 Arrange the scones at least 2 inches apart on the baking sheet. For best results, let the scones rest for 20 to 30 minutes in the fridge or freeze the scones, uncovered, for at least 20 minutes or overnight before baking.

9 Preheat the oven to 375°F.

10 Brush the tops of the scones with the beaten egg and sprinkle with salt and pepper.

11 Bake for 15 to 20 minutes, rotating the sheet 180 degrees every 10 minutes, until the scones are a deep golden brown and sound hollow when tapped on the bottom.

Store wrapped, unbaked scones in the freezer for up to 2 weeks. Baked scones are best eaten the day they are made. Day-old scones can be split, toasted, and spread with butter.

Use the best, sharpest cheddar you can find without breaking the bank. Cabot and Tillamook are two reasonably priced options that work well and are easy to find.

Everything Scones with Whipped Cream Cheese

I was skeptical when my bakers proposed this unlikely pairing. Turns out it's fantastic! Don't skip the whipped cream cheese. It takes the whole recipe to the next level.

Ingredients

Yield: about 12 (2¾-inch) square scones

EVERYTHING SPICE MIX

2 tablespoons	**poppy seeds**	18g
2 tablespoons	**sesame seeds**	18g
2 tablespoons	**granulated garlic or garlic powder**	18g
2 tablespoons	**granulated onion or onion powder**	18g
4 teaspoons	**Maldon salt**	10g

SCONES

3 cups	**all-purpose flour**	360g
1 tablespoon	**sugar**	12g
1½ tablespoons	**baking powder**	18g
¾ teaspoon	**kosher salt**	2.25g
¾ cup (1½ sticks) plus 2 tablespoons	**unsalted butter, cut into ½-inch cubes and chilled**	184g
1 cup	**heavy cream, plus more for brushing**	240g
3 tablespoons	**caraway seeds**	27g

WHIPPED CREAM CHEESE

8 ounces	**cream cheese, softened**	227g
3 tablespoons	**heavy cream**	45g

1 To make the spice mix, combine all the ingredients in a small bowl and rub together with your fingers. Set aside.

Next page

EVERYTHING SCONES WITH WHIPPED CREAM CHEESE, *continued*

2 To make the scones, sift the flour, sugar, and baking powder three times. Transfer to the bowl of a medium food processor. Add the salt and chilled butter and mix for 25 to 30 seconds until the mixture resembles a fine meal.

3 Add the heavy cream and pulse just until it is evenly distributed. The dough should still be crumbly; it should not come together in the food processor.

4 Turn the dough out onto a lightly floured work surface. Scatter the caraway seeds over the dough and knead together by hand until smooth. Roll the dough into a 1¼- to 1½-inch-thick square or rectangle.

5 Punch out the scones using a 2¾-inch square biscuit or cookie cutter. Dip the cutter in flour between each scone.

6 Stack one rimmed baking sheet on top of another and line with parchment paper. (The double panning keeps the bottoms of the scones from overbrowning. This may not be necessary if you have an insulated or extra-heavy baking sheet.)

7 Arrange the scones at least 2 inches apart on the baking sheet. For best results, let the scones rest for 20 to 30 minutes in the fridge or freeze the scones, uncovered, for at least 20 minutes or overnight before baking.

8 Preheat the oven to 425°F.

9 Brush the tops of the scones with cream and sprinkle with the everything spice mix.

10 Bake for 20 to 30 minutes, rotating the sheet 180 degrees every 10 minutes, until the scones are a deep golden brown. They should feel lighter as they bake. Let cool.

11 To make the whipped cream cheese, place the softened cream cheese in the bowl of a stand mixer fitted with the whisk attachment and whip until smooth. With the mixer running, add the heavy cream 1 tablespoon at a time. Continue whipping until light and fluffy.

12 Spread the whipped cream cheese over the scones and serve.

Store wrapped, unbaked scones in the freezer for up to 2 weeks. Baked scones are best eaten the day they are made. Day-old scones can be split, toasted, and spread with whipped cream cheese. Store leftover whipped cream cheese in an airtight container in the refrigerator for up to 1 week. The everything spice mix can be stored in an airtight container at room temperature indefinitely.

Roasted Garlic, Caramelized Onion & Parmesan Scones

Roasting the garlic and caramelizing the onions takes some time, but the depth of flavor they bring out is worth the extra effort.

Ingredients

Yield: about 12 (2¾-inch) square or round scones

4 cups	**all-purpose flour**	480g
1 tablespoon	**sugar**	12g
1 tablespoon	**baking powder**	12g
½ teaspoon	**freshly ground black pepper**	1g
2 tablespoons	**kosher salt**	18g
¼ cup	**Caramelized Onions (page 299)**	~50g
1 head	**Roasted Garlic (page 298)**	~40g
1¼ cups (2½ sticks)	**unsalted butter, cut into ½-inch cubes and chilled**	284g
½ cup	**shredded or grated Parmesan cheese**	50g
1⅓ cups	**heavy cream**	319g
1	**large egg, lightly beaten**	50g

1 Sift the flour, sugar, baking powder, and pepper three times. (If the black pepper is too coarse to pass through a sifter, add it directly to the bowl of the food processor.) Transfer to the bowl of a food processor. Add the salt and caramelized onions. Squeeze the roasted garlic cloves out of their husks into the food processor. Discard any crispy bits. Add the chilled butter and process for 25 to 30 seconds, until the mixture resembles a fine meal.

2 Add the Parmesan cheese and heavy cream and pulse just until it is evenly distributed. The dough should still be crumbly; it should not come together in the food processor.

Next page

ROASTED GARLIC, CARAMELIZED ONION & PARMESAN SCONES, *continued*

3 Turn the dough out onto a lightly floured work surface and knead together by hand until smooth. Roll the dough into a ½-inch-thick rectangle.

4 Punch out the scones using a 2¾-inch square or round biscuit or cookie cutter. Dip the cutter in flour between each scone.

5 Stack one rimmed baking sheet on top of another and line with parchment paper. (The double panning keeps the bottoms of the scones from overbrowning. This may not be necessary if you have an insulated or extra-heavy baking sheet.)

6 Arrange the scones at least 2 inches apart on the baking sheet. For best results, let the scones rest for 20 to 30 minutes in the fridge or freeze the scones, uncovered, for at least 20 minutes or overnight before baking.

7 Preheat the oven to 425°F.

8 Brush the tops of the scones with the beaten egg.

9 Bake for 15 to 20 minutes, rotating the sheet 180 degrees every 10 minutes, until the scones are a deep golden brown and sound hollow when tapped on the bottom.

You don't have to spring for an expensive imported Italian Parmigiano-Reggiano to make these scones delicious, but you don't want to use the dry grated cheese that comes in the green can either. Aim for a good domestic Parmesan. We like BelGioioso because it is made in neighboring Wisconsin, but most grocery stores carry a good, flavorful, mid-range Parm.

PIE·COM
PIE

CHAPTER 3

Biscuits

Biscuits are the original American comfort food. According to a Harris Poll survey, 76 percent of Americans feel happy when they eat biscuits. It's no surprise. Americans have been enjoying them for centuries, though you probably wouldn't be very happy if you were handed an original Colonial-era biscuit. Those first biscuits, called hardtack, were unleavened and dry, designed to survive ocean crossings and military campaigns, not to taste good. Made from just flour, water, and salt, they were baked four times and dried for six months before long voyages. The resulting biscuits were so durable that Revolutionary soldiers used them for postcards.

THE IMPORTANCE OF BISQUICK

Bisquick is a quick and easy shortcut to biscuits, and it is responsible for spreading the love of biscuits across the country. For nearly a century, differences in growing conditions and anti-South bias meant you rarely saw biscuits in cold climates. In the hot South, farmers grew a low-protein soft wheat and milled it into a flour that made light, delicate biscuits but lacked the essential gluten needed to trap the air pockets in yeast-leavened bread. Northern farmers grew a high-protein, hard winter wheat that made great bread but dense, flat biscuits. It didn't help that Northern diners, raised on cold sliced bread with meals, found the Southern practice of eating biscuits hot from the oven uncivilized and unhealthy.

This all changed after a train ride in 1930. Carl Smith, a salesman with General Mills, was headed to San Francisco on business. It was late and he was hungry. The dining car was closed, so he asked his Pullman car porter if he could make him something simple to eat. To his surprise, the porter quickly returned with a plate of hot biscuits. When questioned, the unnamed and uncelebrated porter explained that he made his own biscuit "mix," a combination of flour, lard, baking powder, and salt that he stored in an ice chest. He simply added the liquid ingredients and had biscuits in minutes. Smith took the idea back to General Mills's food scientists, who pioneered a way to make the mix shelf stable. Bisquick hit grocery store shelves the following year, the same year Kentucky bakery owner Lively Willoughby filed a patent for his unlikely invention: ready-to-bake biscuit dough in a refrigerated tube. With that, folks everywhere could make consistently fluffy biscuits in minutes and their popularity spread across the country.

THE STORY OF ANNIE FISHER

In 1927, Annie Fisher was a wealthy woman. She lived in a fourteen-room mansion built to her own specifications. She owned a small empire of rental properties and a fifty-eight-acre farm. While Annie herself was notoriously secretive about finances, a newspaper article at the time estimated her net worth at $150,000, roughly three million dollars today. The most remarkable thing about Annie Fisher was that she was a Black woman in Jim Crow–era Missouri who made her fortune one beaten biscuit at a time.

Annie Knowles Fisher was born in 1867, one of eleven children of formerly enslaved parents. She left school by the third grade and went to work rocking cradles in wealthy white households to support her siblings. While her charges slept, she'd wander down to the kitchen, where the cook was usually happy to put her to work beating biscuits. By the 1890s, Annie was a cook herself, working for a fraternity at the University of Missouri and some of the finest homes in Columbia, Missouri. When one of her employers urged her to start a catering business, she went out on her own. She started small, offering only hot rolls, then pies and cakes, but soon she added whole meals and the "flaky, fluffy, and creamy" biscuits she became known for. Before long, it wasn't a party unless Annie Fisher was cooking. Couples were known to change the dates of their weddings if Annie was busy.

Annie was generous with her recipes. Her recipe for beaten biscuits, in particular, was published many times, though she often joked she couldn't teach the "common sense" required to duplicate them. She also warned they took "elbow grease" and advised you to "go at it from the shoulder, that's the thing that counts" when beating the dough. Annie's beaten biscuit recipe is part of the public domain, so I am publishing it here in case you want to give it a try.

1 quart sifted flour
⅓ cup pure lard
⅓ cup butter
1 cup sweetened water
Salt to taste

The ingredients must be mixed thoroughly, and after the dough becomes about as stiff as pie crust, it must be worked for fifteen minutes.

Note: To make the sweetened water in Annie's recipe, dissolve a small amount of sugar in cold water and add it to the dough after you cut the butter and lard into the flour. Sadly, Annie's preferred sugar-to-water ratio is lost to history (or perhaps it was a closely guarded secret). But similar recipes from the era call for anywhere from no sugar to 3 tablespoons of sugar per 4 cups of flour.

Nonetheless, they were quick to make, using cheap, easy-to-get ingredients, and they became a staple in the new American colonies. Luckily, creative bakers found a way to make them tastier. They added fat, usually lard, and discovered that pounding the biscuits repeatedly tenderized the dough and trapped enough air inside to cause it to rise slightly when baked. The work of making these "beaten biscuits" often fell to enslaved cooks who beat them with rolling pins, hatchets, and even hammers for up to an hour. The process was so labor intensive that serving biscuits in the antebellum South was a sign of prestige and wealth, since it signaled you could afford enough kitchen help to make them for you.

The mid-nineteenth century brought the end of slavery and the invention of baking powder and baking soda. The beaten biscuit fell out of fashion, to be replaced by the flaky, fluffy leavened biscuits we love today.

MIXING BISCUITS

The technique for making these classic buttermilk biscuits is nearly identical to the technique for making scones. To achieve that wonderful flakiness, cut cold butter into your dry ingredients until it resembles a fine meal, add any flavorings like sautéed ramps or cheese, add buttermilk, and knead it all together into a smooth dough. As long as you measure the ingredients correctly, the only way to mess up a batch of biscuits is to overmix it. Just like muffins and scones, overmixed biscuits bake up disappointingly dense, heavy, and flat. Never fear, the three methods you learned to make perfect scones works for biscuits too. The food processor method is detailed in each classic biscuit recipe. Feel free to use any of the three methods you like. For the angel and drop biscuits, follow the recipes as written.

SHAPING CLASSIC BISCUITS

Once you've mixed your dough, pat or roll it into a 1¼- to 1½-inch-thick rectangle. Punch them out with a 2¾-inch square biscuit cutter, dipping the cutter in flour between each cut. For the tallest, fluffiest biscuits, choose metal cutters with thin, sharp edges. In a pinch, a drinking glass with a smooth rim works just fine, too, though the biscuits won't rise quite as high. Be sure to press straight into the dough and pull straight back out. Do not twist. Twisting the cutter seals the edges, keeping the biscuit from rising as high as it should. Biscuits can be baked immediately, but they will be prettier and more tender if they are allowed to rest in the refrigerator for 20 to 30 minutes first. For straighter sides and a more even rise, transfer the rested biscuits to the freezer for at least 20 minutes (or up to 3 days) and bake them off frozen.

Top left: Grate the butter.
Top right: Add the grated butter to the dry ingredients.
Bottom left: Rub the butter into the dry ingredients.
Bottom right: Mix until it resembles a coarse meal.

Classic Buttermilk Biscuits

We serve hundreds of our buttermilk biscuits every week. They are flaky and buttery, with the tanginess of buttermilk and baking soda. Top them with anything from homemade jam to red-eye gravy, or make them into a sandwich using our Biscuit Sandwich Builder on page 166. If you are in a hurry, they can go directly into the oven, but for the prettiest biscuits, freeze them for 20 minutes first. They will rise straighter and spread less.

Ingredients

Yield: about 8 (2¾-inch) square biscuits

3¾ cups	**all-purpose flour**	450g
1 tablespoon	**sugar**	12g
1 tablespoon	**kosher salt**	9g
1 tablespoon	**baking powder**	12g
¾ teaspoon	**baking soda**	3g
1 cup (2 sticks)	**unsalted butter, cut into ½-inch cubes and chilled, plus melted butter for brushing (about ⅓ cup)**	227g
1½ cups	**buttermilk**	340g

1. In a food processor, combine the flour, sugar, salt, baking powder, and baking soda. Add the chilled butter and process for 25 to 30 seconds, until the mixture resembles a fine meal. Add the buttermilk and pulse just until it is evenly distributed. The dough should still be very crumbly; it should not come together in the food processor.
2. Turn the dough out onto a lightly floured work surface and knead together by hand until smooth. Roll the dough into 1¼- to 1½-inch-thick square or rectangle.
3. Punch out the biscuits using a 2¾-inch square biscuit or cookie cutter. Dip the cutter in flour between each biscuit. Gather the dough scraps, knead them together, and roll again. Punch out the remaining biscuits.
4. Line a rimmed baking sheet with parchment paper or coat with cooking spray. Place the biscuits at least 2 inches apart on the baking sheet. For best results, let the biscuits rest in the fridge for 20 to 30 minutes or freeze the biscuits, uncovered, for at least 20 minutes or overnight before baking.

5 Preheat the oven to 425°F.

6 Bake the biscuits for 25 to 30 minutes, until they double in height and turn dark golden brown. Brush the warm biscuits with melted butter and serve immediately.

Store wrapped, unbaked biscuits in the freezer for up to 3 days. Store baked biscuits in an airtight container at room temperature for up to 2 days. Split leftover biscuits and toast in a toaster or 350°F oven.

Ramp Biscuits

Ramps are wild spring onions with a cult following. Chefs prize them for their intense flavor (they taste like extra-buttery leeks with lots of garlic and a handful of chives thrown in) and super-short growing season. Our farmers forage them from early May to mid-June and deliver them to much fanfare. Commercial cultivation is rare, so your best bet is to pick some up at your local farmers' market. Don't be put off by the smell. They are famously stinky when raw, but cooking mellows out the aroma. Olivia Sweets, who runs our Chicago shop, brilliantly developed this recipe to extend ramp season by making a ramp compound butter that freezes beautifully.

Ingredients

Yield: about 6 (2¾-inch) square biscuits

RAMP BUTTER

2 bunches	**ramps**	15g
2 cups (4 sticks)	**unsalted butter, softened to room temperature**	454g
¾ teaspoon	**grated lemon zest**	1.5g
¾ teaspoon	**kosher salt**	2.25g
¼ teaspoon	**freshly ground black pepper**	0.6g

BISCUITS

4 cups	**all-purpose flour**	480g
1 tablespoon	**sugar**	12g
1 tablespoon	**kosher salt**	9g
1 tablespoon	**baking powder**	12g
¾ teaspoon	**baking soda**	3g
½ cup	**grated or shredded Parmesan cheese**	50g
1¼ cups	**buttermilk**	284g
¾ teaspoon	**red pepper flakes**	1.5g
¼ cup (½ stick)	**unsalted butter, melted**	57g

Next page

RAMP BISCUITS, *continued*

1 To make the ramp butter, trim the ramp leaves off the bulb and stem; reserve the bulb and stem for another use. Fill a small bowl with ice water and set aside. Bring a medium saucepan of water to a boil. Add the ramp leaves and press them down into the water. Boil for about 15 seconds, or until the leaves turn bright green. Remove the leaves from the boiling water with a slotted spoon and submerge in the bowl of ice water. Remove the ramps from the ice water and pat dry with paper towels.

2 Roughly chop the leaves; you should have ½ cup.

3 Place the softened butter in the bowl of a stand mixer fitted with the paddle attachment. Mix on medium speed until smooth. Add the ramps, lemon zest, salt, and pepper and mix on low speed until evenly combined, scraping down the sides of the bowl as you go. Form the ramp butter into a rough block, wrap well, and chill in the refrigerator until it is firm and cold. Once chilled, cut 1 cup (227g) of the ramp butter into ½-inch cubes. Store remaining ramp butter in the refrigerator for another use.

4 To make the biscuits, in the bowl of a food processor, combine the flour, sugar, salt, baking powder, baking soda, and Parmesan cheese. Add the chilled ramp butter cubes and process for 25 to 30 seconds, until the mixture resembles a fine meal. Add the buttermilk and pulse just until it is evenly distributed. The dough should still be crumbly; it should not come together in the food processor.

5 Turn the dough out onto a lightly floured work surface. Scatter the red pepper flakes over the dough and knead together by hand until smooth. Roll the dough into a 1¼- to 1½-inch-thick square or rectangle.

6 Punch out the biscuits using a 2¾-inch square biscuit or cookie cutter. Dip the cutter in flour between each biscuit.

7 Line a rimmed baking sheet with parchment paper or coat with cooking spray. Place the biscuits at least 2 inches apart on the baking sheet. For best results, let the biscuits rest in the fridge for 20 to 30 minutes or freeze the biscuits, uncovered, for at least 20 minutes or overnight before baking.

8 Preheat the oven to 375°F.

9 Bake the biscuits for 25 to 30 minutes, until they double in height and turn dark golden brown. Brush warm biscuits with the melted butter and serve immediately.

Ramp butter can be stored in the refrigerator for up to 1 month. Store wrapped, unbaked biscuits in the freezer for up to 3 days. Baked biscuits can be stored in an airtight container at room temperature for up to 2 days. Split leftover biscuits and toast them in a toaster or 350°F oven.

This recipe uses only the leaves, but every part of the ramp is edible. Simply give them a good wash and trim off any remaining string-like roots before cooking. We like to chop up the bulbs, sauté them in butter, and add them to quiche or pickle them to toss on salads.

CLEANING RAMPS

Ramps are notoriously dirty. They grow in wet soil, which gets trapped between its leaves. To clean ramps, submerge them in a bowl of cool water and swish them around to loosen the dirt. Pour off the dirty water and repeat until the water runs clear. Some foragers preclean their ramps and charge an extra dollar or two per pound for the convenience. It is well worth it! Dry ramps by spreading them out on a paper towel–lined baking sheet. You can store ramps in your refrigerator for up to 4 days by wrapping them in a damp paper towel and sealing them in a resealable plastic bag or other airtight container.

Blanching is a cooking technique *that involves briefly cooking fruits and vegetables in boiling water and then immediately plunging them into ice water to stop that cooking. Blanching turns off the enzymes in fruits and vegetables that cause ripening and spoilage. It's especially useful for vegetables that will be frozen, since freezing merely slows down spoilage but does not stop it entirely. Blanching also intensifies and locks in color while preserving flavor and texture. In the case of greens, it takes away any bitterness and tenderizes tough leaves and stems.*

Cheddar-Scallion Biscuits

This is a seasonal recipe that Olivia Sweets developed for our farmers' market stand. Scallion season runs from June through September here in the Midwest, so we enjoy these biscuits once ramp season is over. Scallions, also called green onions, have a bright, crisp, lemony flavor that goes well with a nice sharp cheddar cheese. These biscuits are easy to pair with many different meals and make an excellent base for egg sandwiches.

Ingredients

Yield: about 6 (2¾-inch) square biscuits

1¼ cups (2½ sticks)	**unsalted butter, divided**	284g
4 cups	**all-purpose flour**	480g
1 tablespoon	**sugar**	12g
1 tablespoon	**kosher salt**	9g
1 tablespoon	**baking powder**	12g
¾ teaspoon	**baking soda**	3g
¾ teaspoon	**freshly ground black pepper**	1.5g
2 cups	**grated or shredded cheddar cheese**	226g
2 cups	**chopped scallions**	120g
1¼ cups	**buttermilk**	284g
¼ teaspoon	**granulated garlic**	0.5g

1. Cut 1 cup of the butter into ½-inch cubes and keep refrigerated until ready to use.
2. In the bowl of a food processor, combine the flour, sugar, salt, baking powder, baking soda, black pepper, and cheddar cheese. Add the chilled butter and process for 25 to 30 seconds, until the mixture resembles a fine meal. Add the buttermilk and pulse just until it is evenly distributed. The dough should still be crumbly; it should not come together in the food processor.
3. Turn the dough out onto a lightly floured work surface. Scatter the chopped scallions over the dough and knead it together by hand until smooth. Roll out the dough into a 1¼- to 1½-inch-thick square or rectangle.

Next page

CHEDDAR-SCALLION BISCUITS, *continued*

4 Punch out the biscuits using a 2¾-inch square biscuit or cookie cutter. Dip the cutter in flour between each biscuit. Gather the dough scraps, knead them together, and roll again. Punch out the remaining biscuits.

5 Line a rimmed baking sheet with parchment paper or coat with cooking spray. Place the biscuits at least 2 inches apart on the baking sheet. For best results, let the biscuits rest in the fridge for 20 to 30 minutes or freeze the biscuits, uncovered, for at least 20 minutes or overnight before baking.

6 Preheat the oven to 425°F.

7 Bake the biscuits for 25 to 30 minutes, until they double in height and turn dark golden brown.

8 In a small saucepan, melt the remaining ¼ cup butter over medium-low heat. Whisk in the granulated garlic until dissolved.

9 Brush the warm biscuits with the garlic butter and serve immediately.

Store wrapped, unbaked biscuits in the freezer for up to 3 days. Store baked biscuits in an airtight container at room temperature for up to 2 days. Split leftover biscuits and toast them in a toaster or 350°F oven.

Cornmeal Biscuits

These biscuits are extra light and tender with a subtle cornmeal crunch.
I like to cut them out in smaller circles to maximize the buttery-crust-to-fluffy-crumb ratio. Serve them with tomato soup, a spoonful of honey, or as the base for a country Benedict with sautéed greens and an over-easy egg.

Ingredients

Yield: 8 to 10 (2¾-inch) square or (3-inch) round biscuits or about 12 (2½-inch) round biscuits

2½ cups	**all-purpose flour**	300g
1¼ cups	**medium-grind yellow cornmeal**	172g
1 tablespoon	**sugar**	12g
1 tablespoon	**kosher salt**	9g
1 tablespoon	**baking powder**	12g
¾ teaspoon	**baking soda**	3g
1¼ cups (2½ sticks)	**unsalted butter, cut into ½-inch cubes and chilled, plus melted butter for brushing (about ⅓ cup)**	283g
1½ cups	**buttermilk**	340g

1 In the bowl of a food processor, combine the flour, cornmeal, sugar, salt, baking powder, and baking soda. Add the chilled butter and process for 25 to 30 seconds, until the mixture resembles a fine meal. Add the buttermilk and pulse just until it is evenly distributed. The dough should still be crumbly; it should not come together in the food processor.

2 Turn the dough out onto a lightly floured work surface and knead together by hand until smooth. Roll the dough into a 1¼- to 1½-inch-thick square or rectangle.

3 Punch out the biscuits using a 2¾-inch square biscuit or cookie cutter. Dip the cutter in flour between each biscuit. Gather the dough scraps, knead them together, and roll again. Punch out the remaining biscuits.

Next page

CORNMEAL BISCUITS, *continued*

4 Line a rimmed baking sheet with parchment paper or coat with cooking spray. Place the biscuits at least 2 inches apart on the baking sheet. For best results, let the biscuits rest in the fridge for 20 to 30 minutes or freeze the biscuits, uncovered, for at least 20 minutes or overnight before baking.

5 Preheat the oven to 425°F.

6 Bake the biscuits for 25 to 30 minutes, until they double in height and turn golden, with a few light brown patches. Brush the warm biscuits with melted butter and serve immediately.

Store wrapped, unbaked biscuits in the freezer for up to 3 days. Store baked biscuits in an airtight container at room temperature for up to 2 days. Split leftover biscuits and toast in a toaster or 350°F oven.

Pumpkin Biscuits

This savory biscuit has a delicate pumpkin flavor and a pretty orange hue. An obvious choice for your Thanksgiving table, it also makes a great base for sandwiches. Try it topped with cranberry sauce and leftover turkey. For breakfast, add a spoonful of honey or sorghum butter.

Ingredients

Yield: about 10 (2½-inch) round biscuits

1½ cups (3 sticks)	**unsalted butter, plus melted butter for brushing**	340g
4 cups	**all-purpose flour**	480g
¼ cup	**packed dark brown sugar**	53g
2 tablespoons	**baking powder**	24g
2 tablespoons	**kosher salt**	18g
1¼ teaspoons	**pumpkin pie spice**	3g
1 teaspoon	**baking soda**	4g
1 teaspoon	**freshly ground black pepper**	2g
1¼ cups	**buttermilk**	284g
1 cup	**canned pumpkin puree**	245g

1. Grate the butter using the shredding side of a box grater (the wide side with ¼-inch holes). Set aside in the freezer until ready to use.
2. In a medium bowl, whisk together the flour, brown sugar, baking powder, salt, pumpkin pie spice, baking soda, and pepper. Toss the frozen grated butter in the dry ingredients to incorporate. Work the butter into the flour mixture with your fingers until it resembles a coarse meal.
3. Make a well in the center and pour in the buttermilk and pumpkin puree. Mix the dough gently by hand in the bowl until it just comes together.
4. Turn the dough out onto a lightly floured work surface and knead until smooth. Roll out the dough into a 1¼- to 1½-inch-thick rectangle.
5. Punch out the biscuits with a 2½-inch round biscuit or cookie cutter. Dip the cutter in flour between each biscuit. Gather the dough scraps, knead them together, and roll again. Punch out the remaining biscuits.

6 Line a rimmed baking sheet with parchment paper or coat with cooking spray. Place the biscuits at least 2 inches apart on the baking sheet. For best results, let the biscuits rest in the fridge for 20 to 30 minutes or freeze the biscuits, uncovered, for at least 20 minutes or overnight before baking.

7 Preheat the oven to 425°F.

8 Bake the biscuits for 15 to 20 minutes, until the biscuits double in height and the tops turn a light golden brown. Brush the warm biscuits with melted butter and serve immediately.

Store wrapped, unbaked biscuits in the freezer for up to 3 days. Store baked biscuits in an airtight container at room temperature for up to 2 days. Split leftover biscuits and toast in a toaster or 350°F oven.

Sorghum and Butter

Classic Biscuit Toppings

What's better than a warm biscuit straight from the oven? That same biscuit with one of these classic biscuit toppings! All of these combinations have stood the comfort food test of time. For more classic pairings, top your biscuits with Apple Butter (page 274) or homemade Strawberry Jam (page 279).

SORGHUM AND BUTTER

Don't confuse this with French-based compound butter. It is pure Americana. In many Southern and Midwestern houses, the jar of sorghum hits the table as soon as biscuits come out of the oven. It's customary to pour a big puddle of syrup on your plate and stir in a knob of butter before spreading it all on a hot biscuit. My mother-in-law still keeps a jar on hand and after some consultation, we determined that two parts sorghum to one part butter is a good place to start. Feel free to adjust the ratio to your taste. Whipping it in a mixer makes it a bit fancy.

Ingredients

Yield: about 1 cup

5 tablespoons	**unsalted butter, softened to room temperature**	113g
⅔ cup	**sorghum syrup**	330g

1 Combine the butter and sorghum syrup in the bowl of a stand mixer fitted with the whisk attachment. Mix on medium speed until the ingredients are combined and the mixture is fluffy.

Store in an airtight container in the refrigerator for up to 1 week. Let come to room temperature or re-whip before serving.

PIMENTO CHEESE SPREAD

Our savory chef, Melissa Humphrey, first developed this recipe for a traditional sandwich, but it is no surprise I like it best on a biscuit. You can eat it by itself or layer it with sliced bacon, ham, turkey, chicken, egg, tomato, avocado—you get the idea!

Ingredients

Yield: about 2 cups

½ cup	**cream cheese, softened**	113g
½ teaspoon	**kosher salt**	1.5g
½ teaspoon	**freshly ground black pepper**	1g
¼ cup	**mayonnaise**	57g
1 tablespoon	**whole-grain Dijon mustard**	15g
1 cup	**grated sharp cheddar cheese**	113g
2 tablespoons	**chopped jarred roasted red peppers**	30g

1 Combine the cream cheese, salt, and pepper in the bowl of a stand mixer fitted with the paddle attachment and mix on medium speed until soft, fluffy, and smooth. Add mayonnaise and mix until smooth. Add the mustard and cheddar cheese and mix until smooth. Remove the bowl from the mixer and fold in the roasted red peppers by hand.

Store in an airtight container in the refrigerator for up to 1 week.

SAUSAGE GRAVY

Like so many delicious things, putting gravy on biscuits was invented out of necessity. Water or milk, pork sausage, and flour were abundant and cheap, and the resulting dish is tasty and (there's no way around it) high-calorie—perfect for feeding Revolutionary War soldiers and later, laborers at the sawmills of Southern Appalachia. It is often also called sawmill gravy.

Yield: about 6 servings

3 cups	**whole milk, plus more as needed**	720g
22	**fresh sage leaves, divided**	10g
1 pound	**bulk pork breakfast sausage**	454g
¼ cup (½ stick)	**unsalted butter**	57g
1½ teaspoons	**kosher salt**	4.5g
¼ cup	**all-purpose flour**	30g
½ teaspoon	**red pepper flakes**	1g
⅛ teaspoon	**ground nutmeg**	0.25g
Generous pinch	**garlic powder**	
Generous pinch	**onion powder**	
¾ teaspoon	**freshly ground black pepper**	1.5g

1. In a medium saucepan, heat the milk to just below a boil (small bubbles will form around the sides of the saucepan). Tear 10 of the sage leaves in half and add them to the milk. Remove the pan from the heat, cover, and let steep for 15 minutes.
2. Meanwhile, in a medium skillet, brown the sausage over medium-high heat, breaking it into small chunks with a wooden spoon as it cooks, until no longer pink, about 10 minutes. Remove the pan from the heat.
3. Strain the sage-infused milk into a pitcher or large measuring cup.
4. Melt the butter in a large saucepan over medium heat. When the butter starts to sizzle, add the remaining 12 sage leaves. Fry the leaves in the butter until crispy but not brown, 30 to 35 seconds. Use a fork or slotted spoon to transfer the sage leaves to a paper towel–lined plate. Immediately sprinkle with the salt.

Next page

SAUSAGE GRAVY, *continued*

5 Turn the heat down to medium. Add the flour to the melted butter to make a roux. Whisk until pale yellow, about 2 minutes. Slowly whisk in the milk. Bring the milk to a boil, whisking constantly. Turn the heat down to a simmer and continue whisking until thick. Stir in the sausage, red pepper flakes, nutmeg, garlic powder, onion powder, and black pepper. Adjust the seasoning and thickness to taste. Add additional whole milk to thin the gravy as desired.

6 Serve warm gravy over lightly toasted biscuits. Garnish with the fried sage leaves.

Store in the refrigerator for up to 4 days or in the freezer for up to 4 months.

People are passionate about the thickness of their gravy. Some folks think you should be able to stand a spoon up in it, while others want it just thick enough to stick to a biscuit. I prefer a thicker gravy myself and do not consider this a moral failing, no matter what certain members of my family will tell you. You may choose to adjust this recipe to your liking, and we will love you for it.

RED-EYE GRAVY

Red-eye gravy is more of a thin sauce than what we Northerners would call gravy. It's made by pan-frying salty, funky country ham and deglazing the pan with strong coffee. It is surprisingly delicious, a triumph of make-do cooking that's been a staple in the South for more than two hundred years. Modern versions add butter for body and sweeteners, like honey or even Coca-Cola, to balance the coffee's bitter edge. Soaking the ham in water before cooking mellows the saltiness. If you're a true Southerner, feel free to skip this step.

Red-eye gravy probably gets its name from its appearance. As it cools, the coffee sinks to the bottom, leaving a circle of grease on top that resembles a red eye. Some folks say President Andrew Jackson coined the term when he was a US Army general and had a camp cook who drank too much. The story goes that for breakfast one morning he requested ham with gravy as red as his hungover cook's eyes. Others say the gravy was named for the sleep-deprived farmers who rose before dawn and relied on the extra jolt of caffeine in the gravy to start their day.

RED-EYE GRAVY, *continued*

Yield: about 2 cups

8 ounces	**country ham, sliced thin**	227g
2 tablespoons	**unsalted butter**	28g
¾ cup	**strong coffee**	180g
¼ cup	**water**	60g
1 tablespoon	**sorghum**	21g
¾ teaspoon	**freshly ground black pepper**	1.5g

1 Place the country ham in a shallow bowl or baking dish and cover with cool tap water. Let soak for 30 to 60 minutes at room temperature or overnight in the refrigerator. Remove the ham from the water and pat dry. Cut a few ½-inch slits around the edges of the ham slices to keep them from curling up when cooked.

2 Heat the butter in a large cast-iron or other heavy skillet over medium-high heat until bubbling. Add the ham slices and fry, adjusting the heat as necessary, until the ham is bright pink and just starting to brown, about 3 minutes per side for 2-ounce "biscuit slices"; thick-cut slices will take longer.

3 Transfer the ham slices to a plate and invert another plate on top to keep the ham warm while you make the gravy.

4 Turn the heat down to medium and pour the coffee into the skillet, scraping up any ham bits from the bottom with a wooden spoon or spatula. Add the water, sorghum, and black pepper and simmer, stirring occasionally, until reduced by half, about 8 minutes.

Red-eye gravy is traditionally made in small batches as needed, but if you do have any left over, you can store it in the refrigerator for up to 5 days or in the freezer for up to 2 months.

To get the full, rich, distinctive flavor from your red-eye gravy, you must start with authentic country ham, and unless you live south of the Ohio, that almost certainly means ordering it by mail (see page 11). Even in Chicago, the "hog butcher to the world," I was met with blank stares when I asked for country ham. The good news is there are lots of delicious options. If you're a baffled Northerner like me, see the sidebar for some tips.

Red-Eye Gravy (page 152)

COUNTRY HAM

*Country ham dates back to the first American colony when settlers at Jamestown, Virginia, combined European and Native American techniques to preserve meat. Country hams are dry-cured, meaning they are rubbed with a mixture of salt, sugar, and spices and sometimes smoked. Then, they are aged anywhere from three months to two years. It turns out one thing the unlucky settlers had going for them was they had landed squarely in what became known as the ham belt, a band running around the globe where the climate is perfect for producing ham, not so cold that the hams freeze in winter or so hot that it spoils in summer. The band runs through the top country ham–making states of Virginia, Kentucky, Tennessee, and North Carolina to Parma, Italy (prosciutto); Bayonne, France (*jambon de Bayonne*); the Iberian peninsula in Spain and Portugal (*jamón ibérico*); and Jinhua, China, where they make the legendary dry-cured Jinhua ham from a one-thousand-year-old recipe.*

City hams came about with the invention of refrigeration. They are wet-cured using a saltwater brine. Hams are either submerged or injected with the brine and refrigerated to preserve them while they cure. For injected hams, curing can take as few as two or three days, making them much cheaper to produce and more affordable to purchase. Once cured, hams are smoked over fruitwood and almost always fully or partially cooked. The resulting ham is moist and tender with a less intense, less salty flavor than country ham.

Country ham is pricey. Curing and aging the meat takes time, and the longer the ham cures, the more it will cost (and the better it will taste). It is also a regional delicacy that can't be produced everywhere. Think of it as the prosciutto of Appalachia and expect to pay fifteen to thirty dollars per pound or more. You can buy it cooked or uncooked. You'll need the uncooked version to get the rich pan drippings for the gravy.

Country ham comes in many sizes, from whole hams packed in muslin bags to vacuum-sealed slices. For this recipe, four 2-ounce "biscuit slices" work well. They are sliced thin, so they cook quickly and stay tender. Plus, they're the perfect size for biscuit sandwiches. An 8-ounce bone-in center-cut slice, also called a ham steak, is another good option. It is terrific served with runny eggs, and the bone marrow makes the gravy extra rich.

Country ham has a funky, sweet, fruity aroma much like a washed-rind cheese and a strong, fruity, nutty, salty flavor to match. Don't be alarmed if your ham arrives at room temperature. Remember, country ham was invented to preserve meat without refrigeration. Follow the package instructions for storage.

CHOCOLATE GRAVY

Yup, I said chocolate gravy. If you're not in the know, combining the words chocolate and gravy sounds questionable. Still, this buttery, cocoa powder–based chocolate sauce has been a breakfast staple poured over hot biscuits for generations in the Ozark and Appalachian regions of the Deep South. Whether the biscuits are split and served open-faced or crumbled into the sauce is a matter of family loyalty. Chocolate gravy is also known as sopping chocolate, and you'll want to sop up every last drop.

Yield: about 6 servings

1 cup	**sugar**	200g
¾ cup	**cocoa powder, preferably Dutch-processed**	64g
3 tablespoons	**all-purpose flour**	24g
2 cups	**whole milk**	454g
Pinch	**kosher salt**	
3 tablespoons	**unsalted butter, softened to room temperature**	42g

1 Whisk together the sugar, cocoa powder, and flour in a small, heavy-bottomed saucepan or cast-iron skillet over medium heat. Slowly pour in about half of the milk, whisking continuously to make a smooth paste. Whisk in the rest of the milk. Turn the heat up to medium-high and cook, whisking constantly, until thickened, about 5 minutes. Add the salt. Whisk in the butter until melted. Serve immediately.

Store leftovers in an airtight container in the refrigerator for up to 4 days. Fun fact: cold chocolate gravy = chocolate pudding!

HISTORY OF CHOCOLATE GRAVY

The origins of chocolate gravy are a mystery. According to the Oxford Encyclopedia of Food and Drink in America, *it was a traditional part of Melungeon cuisine—the Melungeons being a near-mythical mixed-race tribe that, according to lore, lived in isolation in remote parts of Appalachia. The theory is that they carried the exotic recipe with them from Spanish colonies on the East Coast of what is now the United States in the sixteenth and seventeenth centuries. New research, however, suggests the Melungeons were not a single ethnic group at all but many different mixed-race families who moved to remote Appalachia to escape the prejudice of the day, and the term Melungeon was a slur used to refer to anyone of mixed race. Another theory, also from the* Oxford Encyclopedia, *suggests that trade between Spanish-held Louisiana and the Tennessee Valley introduced Mexican-style drinking chocolate to the region, which locals quickly adapted to their traditional way of eating and poured it over biscuits. My vote, though, goes to Fred Sauceman, associate professor of Appalachian studies at East Tennessee State University, who says that chocolate gravy is a more recent invention. When Milton Hershey introduced canned, shelf-stable cocoa powder in the early 1900s, home cooks seized on a way to make something cheap, quick, and delicious for their families. Recipes for chocolate gravy started showing up in cookbooks and became something of a craze in the Depression-era 1930s.*

Sticky Biscuits

Sisters Maria and Anayelli, longtime Hoosier Mama bakers, used to make these as kitchen treats out of the biscuit dough left over after the second roll. One year, we passed them out to customers in the Thanksgiving pie line. When the customers returned the following week requesting them, we put sticky biscuits on the menu. The sticky part refers to the dough, your hands, and perhaps your apron after being dunked in melted butter and rolled in sugar. The more butter and sugar, the better.

Ingredients

Yield: 5 to 6, depending on the amount of scrap dough

	Remaining dough from biscuits	
1 cup	**sugar**	200g
2 tablespoons	**ground cinnamon or pumpkin pie spice**	16g
½ cup (1 stick)	**unsalted butter, melted**	113g
1 recipe	**Simple Glaze (page 291), for finishing**	

1. Preheat the oven to 375°F. Line a rimmed baking sheet with parchment paper.
2. Roll the scrap biscuit dough 1¼ to 1½ inches thick. Punch out the biscuits using a 2¾-inch square biscuit cutter. Cut each biscuit in half diagonally so you have two triangles.
3. In a medium bowl, mix the sugar and cinnamon together until well mixed. Dunk the biscuit triangles in the melted butter for 5 or 6 seconds, then toss immediately in the cinnamon sugar.
4. Place the biscuits on the lined baking sheet, leaving lots of space between them.
5. Bake until cooked through but still moist, 15 to 20 minutes. Let the biscuits cool completely, then drizzle with simple glaze.

Sticky biscuits are best eaten within a few hours of baking.

Biscuit French Toast Casserole

This casserole is a luxe way to use up stale biscuits. If you have frozen biscuits that have lost their oomph from too much time in the freezer, bake them off. They'll work great for this, too. Customize by adding chocolate chips, dried fruit, and/or nuts. A combination of dried cherries and chocolate chips is my favorite addition.

Ingredients

Yield: about 12 servings

12	**large eggs**	600g
¾ cup	**sugar, plus more for sprinkling**	150g
Pinch	**kosher salt**	
1½ teaspoons	**ground cinnamon**	3.9g
½ teaspoon	**ground nutmeg**	1g
3 ½ cups	**heavy cream**	840g
½ cup	**whole milk**	120g
2 teaspoons	**vanilla paste**	10g
7 or 8	**stale biscuits**	525–600g
1 cup	**semisweet chocolate chips, dried cherries, or nuts (optional)**	170g
	Warm maple syrup, for serving (optional)	

1. Butter a 3-quart casserole dish.
2. In a large bowl, whisk together the eggs, sugar, salt, cinnamon, and nutmeg. Add the heavy cream, milk, and vanilla and whisk until well combined.
3. Working from the top down, cut each biscuit into three roughly 1-inch-thick slices. Arrange the biscuit slices in overlapping rows in the casserole dish. Fill in any spaces on the sides with the remaining biscuits. Scatter the chocolate chips over the biscuits, if using.

4 Pour the egg mixture over the biscuits. Press the biscuits down into the egg mixture with the back of a spoon. The dish will be very full. Cover the dish with aluminum foil and refrigerate overnight.

5 Preheat the oven to 300°F.

6 Uncover and bake the casserole for 45 minutes. Remove it from the oven. Press the biscuits down into the liquid with a wooden spoon or heatproof spatula. Run a spatula between the biscuits and the sides of the pan. Return the casserole to the oven and bake for 15 more minutes. Sprinkle sugar over the top of the casserole, then bake for about 10 more minutes, or until the top is lightly browned and the center is just set. Serve with warm maple syrup, if using.

Store the casserole, covered, in the refrigerator for up to 2 days. To reheat individual servings, place a bowlful in the microwave next to a small dish of water. Heat for about 1 minute (microwaves will vary), until warmed through.

The flavor bump from grating fresh nutmeg is worth the extra effort. Use a Microplane or specialized nutmeg grater.

Biscuit Cobblers

This is a great way to use up scrap dough that's left over when you roll out biscuits. The biscuits soak up the yummy fruit juices, tenderizing them so you don't need to worry about overworked dough. It's also a great way to pull together a quick seasonal dessert in a hurry. You can whip up a batch of biscuit dough on the fly and top the cobbler immediately or use any biscuits you have stocked in the freezer. Just set them out on the counter to thaw until they are soft enough to work with. It shouldn't take more than half an hour. The toppings are a great place to play with different flavors and customize the recipe to your taste or the fruit you use. Chopped candied ginger is fantastic with peaches, and ground pink peppercorn makes berry flavors pop. The biscuits rely on the topping for sweetness, and I think it is just about perfect with a big scoop of vanilla ice cream. If you are making biscuit dough just for a cobbler and want something sweeter, add an extra tablespoon of sugar.

Cobblers are versatile. You can make them just about any shape or size you like. The trick is to fill your pan or pans two-thirds full with cooked fruit and cover most of the fruit with biscuit dough—easy! As a rough guide, I use 2½ ounces of dough (about half a biscuit) for every ½ cup of fruit.

Yield: 4 individual cobblers

2 tablespoons	**packed dark brown sugar**	28g
2 tablespoons	**pecans, lightly toasted and chopped**	14g
¼ teaspoon	**ground cinnamon**	~0.5g
1 recipe	**Blueberry Cobbler Filling (page 285) or Cherry Cobbler Filling (page 286)**	
2	**Classic Buttermilk Biscuits (page 134), unbaked**	
2 tablespoons	**milk or heavy cream**	30g

1 Preheat the oven to 350°F.

2 Combine the brown sugar, pecans, and cinnamon in a small bowl and rub with your fingers to combine.

3 Arrange four 8-ounce ramekins on a rimmed baking sheet. Fill each ramekin with ½ cup cobbler filling. Smooth the filling flat. Cover the cobbler filling with one large or several smaller pieces of biscuit dough, about 2½ ounces per ramekin. Brush the dough with milk and generously top with the pecan mixture.

4 Bake for 25 to 30 minutes, until the biscuits are puffed, baked through, and lightly browned. The cobbler filling will bubble up around the biscuits. Lift a corner of a biscuit to check for doneness. The biscuits should be moist but set.

Store baked cobblers, wrapped, in the refrigerator overnight. Reheat in a 350°F oven for 15 minutes. Cover the ramekins with aluminum foil if the tops begin to overbrown.

BAKING YOUR COBBLER IN MASON JARS

At the shop, we struggled with a way to serve a cobbler that was both pretty (cobbler is messy by definition—it literally means to cobble together) and portable. Then we hit upon 8-ounce wide-mouth mason jars. They are oven-safe in a water bath, inexpensive, and adorable. The glass sides show off the pretty fruit filling; you can even put the tops on for transport. Follow the recipe above, substituting mason jars for ramekins, but place the mason jars in a baking dish. Fill the dish with water so it is at least halfway up the sides of the jars. Once the cobblers are baked, let them cool to room temperature in the water bath. Be sure to double-check that the jars are food-safe and heat-resistant. The popularity of the farmhouse aesthetic introduced many solely decorative items. Kerr, Ball, and Weck are good brands to try, though perfectly good, cheaper options exist. Make sure to read the label. Be especially suspicious of anything in a decorative color.

Biscuit Sandwiches

"Slap some bacon on a biscuit and let's go! We're burnin' daylight."

—JOHN WAYNE

Sadly, history does not recognize the first person to put eggs, cheese, and fixins between two biscuit halves and call it a sandwich. If it were up to me, there would be monuments in their honor. It's an amazingly satisfying meal any time of day, and the only thing that makes eating breakfast on the go feel like an indulgence.

The chart on page 166 shows some biscuit sammie combinations our customers love. You can make just one or a whole sheet pan's worth. To make each biscuit sandwich, split a biscuit and put the top and bottom halves, cut sides up, on a rimmed baking sheet. Add the "Stack 1" toppings to the biscuit top and the "Stack 2" toppings on the biscuit bottom. To swap out a Fat Egg for over-easy, sunny-side-up, or poached, reduce the baking time to 10 minutes and add the egg when ready to serve.

Facing page: The Marroz Special (page 166)

BISCUIT SANDWICH BUILDER

	Stack 1	Stack 2	Instructions
Egg, Bacon & Cheddar	• 2 slices cooked bacon • 1½ slices cheddar cheese • Biscuit top	• 1 square Fat Egg (page 168) • 1½ slices cheddar cheese • Biscuit bottom	Bake at 350°F for 15 minutes, then close and serve.
Sausage & Leek	• 2 slices butterkäse cheese • Biscuit top	• 2 slices butterkäse cheese • 1 (2-ounce) cooked sausage patty • 1 tablespoon Melted Leeks (page 169) • Biscuit bottom	Bake at 350°F for 15 minutes, then close and serve.
Egg, Mushroom & Gruyère	• 1 slice Gruyère cheese • 2 tablespoons Roasted Mushrooms (page 172) • Biscuit top	• 1 square Fat Egg (page 168) • 1 slice Gruyère cheese • 2 tablespoons Roasted Mushrooms (page 172) • Biscuit bottom	Bake at 350°F for 15 minutes, then close and serve.
Egg, Spinach & Caramelized Onions	• 1 square Fat Egg (page 168) • 2 slices Gruyère cheese • Biscuit top	• 2 tablespoons each Sautéed Winter Spinach (page 171) and Caramelized Onion Filling (page 299) • 2 slices Gruyère cheese • Biscuit bottom	Bake at 350°F for 15 minutes, then close and serve.
Green Eggs & Ham	• 1½ ounces Duroc ham • 1 slice Havarti cheese • Biscuit top	• 1 slice Havarti cheese • 1 square Green Fat Egg (page 168) • 2 tablespoons Pesto Mayo (page 177) • Biscuit bottom	Bake at 350°F for 15 minutes, then close and serve.
The Marroz Special	• 1½ slices cheddar cheese • 1 (2-ounce) sausage patty • Biscuit top	• 1½ slices cheddar cheese • 1 (2-ounce) sausage patty • Biscuit bottom	Bake at 350°F for 15 minutes, then drizzle each side with 1 teaspoon honey. Serve open-faced.
The Remy	• 1 square Fat Egg (page 168) • 2 slices Gruyère cheese • Biscuit top	• 2 tablespoons Ratatouille (page 174) • 2 slices Gruyère cheese • Biscuit bottom	Bake at 350°F for 15 minutes, then close and serve.
Egg, Asparagus & Gruyère	• 1 square Fat Egg (page 168) • 2 slices Gruyère cheese • Biscuit top	• 3 ounces Roasted Asparagus (page 170) • 2 slices Gruyère cheese • Biscuit bottom	Bake at 350°F for 15 minutes, then close and serve.

Egg, Bacon & Cheddar biscuit sandwich (page 166), featuring a Fat Egg (page 168)

FAT EGG

At the pie shop, we don't have time or space to poach or fry eggs to order for biscuit sandwiches, so founding savory chef Allison Scott came up with this delicious solution. We whisk together eggs, sour cream or crème fraîche, and heavy cream (this is the fat part), then bake it in the oven. The result is a fluffy, creamy omelet cake perfect for cutting into biscuit-size squares. If you're planning brunch for a crowd, make the fat egg a day ahead and store the egg patties in the refrigerator until ready to build and heat the sandwiches. Fat egg scraps are delicious folded into breakfast burritos or tossed on salads instead of hard-boiled eggs.

Yield: 9 (2½-inch) egg squares

15	**large eggs**	750g
¾ cup	**sour cream or crème fraîche**	180g
¾ cup	**heavy cream**	180g
2 tablespoons	**all-purpose flour**	15g
1½ teaspoons	**kosher salt**	4.5g
1 teaspoon	**freshly ground black pepper**	2g

1. Preheat the oven to 300°F. Liberally spray a 9 × 13-inch baking dish with cooking spray.
2. Crack the eggs into a medium bowl and whisk to break up the yolks. Whisk in the sour cream and heavy cream. Sift the flour over the egg mixture. Add the salt and pepper and whisk until the ingredients are well combined.
3. Pour the mixture through a fine-mesh sieve into the prepared baking dish.
4. Bake for 30 to 35 minutes, until the edges are puffed and the eggs feel firm when pressed in the middle. If you are using the eggs immediately, cut the eggs once the pan is cool enough to handle; if making ahead, you can cool the eggs to room temperature first.
5. Punch out the egg squares using the same cutter you used for the biscuits, or cut the eggs into squares using a paring knife. Gently lift the egg squares from the pan using an offset spatula or food turner and transfer them to a plate. Cooled egg patties can be stacked to save space.

Store in the refrigerator, wrapped in plastic or in a resealable bag, for up to 3 days. Do not freeze.

Turn these into green eggs by whisking 1/4 cup Nut-Free Pesto (page 176) into the strained egg mixture before baking.

MELTED LEEKS

Melted leeks are the low-key star of our Sausage & Leek biscuit sandwich (page 166). This subtle cousin of onions and garlic turns buttery and sweet when allowed to cook low and slow. A hint of chive-iness means it holds its own with bigger flavors. Leeks retain a lot of the soil they were grown in, so don't rush the cleaning process (see sidebar).

Yield: about ¼ cup

1 teaspoon	**unsalted butter**	5g
1 teaspoon	**extra-virgin olive oil**	4.5g
½ cup	**sliced leeks (⅛ to ¼ inch thick)**	43g
	kosher salt and freshly ground black pepper to taste	

1 Melt the butter and olive oil in a small sauté pan over medium heat. Add the leeks and cook, stirring often, for 2 to 3 minutes. Cover the pan, turn the heat down to low, and continue cooking until the leeks are soft and golden, about 10 minutes. They should not brown.

2 Spread the leeks onto a plate or baking sheet to cool and season with salt and pepper.

Store in an airtight container in the refrigerator for up to 5 days.

CLEANING LEEKS

To clean leeks, cut off the stringy roots and green tops (reserve the green tops for making stock). Remove any white outer leaves that feel dried out or tough. Slice the leeks in half lengthwise and cut each half into ⅛- to ¼-inch half-moon slices. Place the leek slices in a large bowl of cold water. Swish the leeks around in the water for 30 seconds. Let them stand in the water for 20 minutes, letting dirt and sand fall to the bottom of the bowl. Pour into a strainer and rinse under cool running water. Dry the leeks in a salad spinner or pat dry with paper towels.

ROASTED ASPARAGUS

In the summer, when the asparagus crop is strong, our farmers offer us the choice of green or purple vegetables with thick or thin stalks. All options are delicious, but it comes down to personal preference. The baking times in this recipe are calculated for asparagus with medium stalks—the kind you are most likely to find at the grocery store. Adjust the roasting time accordingly if yours are thinner or thicker.

Yield: about 4 servings

1 pound	**asparagus, woody ends snapped off**	454g
¼ cup	**extra-virgin olive oil, plus more if needed**	55g
Generous pinch	**kosher salt, plus more to taste**	
Generous pinch	**freshly ground black pepper, plus more to taste**	

1. Preheat the oven to 400°F.
2. Toss the asparagus on a rimmed baking sheet with the olive oil, salt, and pepper. Roast for 10 minutes. Stir. Add another tablespoon of olive oil if the asparagus sticks to the pan. Roast for 3 to 5 more minutes, until the asparagus is bright green and al dente. Season to taste with additional salt and pepper.

Store in an airtight container in the refrigerator for up to 3 days.

SAUTÉED WINTER SPINACH

Winter spinach is a cold-hardy variety planted in the early fall for harvest in the winter and spring. The plants survive freezing temperatures by converting some of their starches to sugar, creating a natural antifreeze and a wonderfully sweet, complex flavor. The leaves are big and beefy enough to withstand cooking. Look for winter spinach at farmers' markets and in CSA boxes. If you can't find winter spinach, substitute mature spinach with large leaves.

Yield: about 1 cup cooked spinach

2 tablespoons	**unsalted butter**	28g
2 tablespoons	**extra-virgin olive oil**	28g
2 cloves	**garlic, minced**	10g
1 pound	**winter spinach, cleaned and stemmed**	454g
¾ teaspoon	**kosher salt**	2.25g
½ teaspoon	**freshly ground black pepper**	1g

1 Heat the butter and olive oil in a heavy-bottomed skillet or sauté pan over medium-high heat until the butter melts and the mixture starts to bubble. Add the garlic and cook until fragrant, about 30 seconds. Add the spinach and toss to coat in the fat. Sprinkle with the salt and pepper. Sauté until the leaves turn bright green and cook down by one-half to one-third, no more than 2 minutes. The leaves should retain some shape and texture. Serve right away or spread onto a rimmed baking sheet to cool.

Store in an airtight container in the refrigerator for up to 3 days.

MUSHROOMS, TWO WAYS

When our Evanston shop opened, we sautéed all the mushrooms for our mushroom and egg biscuit sandwiches in small batches on our two induction burners. As the sandwiches took off, we needed more and more mushrooms and the bakers got more and more impatient waiting for a free burner to make custards and pastry creams. We knew we needed to get the same delicious results in big batches, so the oven-roasted mushroom recipe was born, freeing us up to accomplish other tasks while the mushrooms slow-roasted in the oven. Both methods provide delicious results. If you are cooking for one or two people, turning on the oven and getting out a baking dish seems silly. If you are serving a crowd or want to have all your ingredients ready ahead of time, why not throw everything in a baking dish and spend an hour prepping the rest of the meal or reading a book? Feel free to use any combination of mushroom varieties you like or have on hand. Leftover mushrooms are fantastic when cooked into frittatas, tossed with pasta, or served as a garnish with steak or chicken.

SMALL-BATCH PAN-SAUTÉED MUSHROOMS

Yield: about 1 cup

2 tablespoons	**unsalted butter**	28g
1 tablespoon	**extra-virgin olive oil**	14g
8 ounces	**cremini mushrooms or a mix of your favorite varieties, stemmed and cut into ¼-inch slices**	227g
1 clove	**garlic, finely chopped**	5g
1 teaspoon	**chopped fresh thyme**	1g
Generous pinch	**kosher salt**	
Generous pinch	**freshly ground black pepper**	
	Grated zest of 1 small lemon	

1 Heat the butter and olive oil in a medium heavy-bottomed sauté pan over medium-high heat until shimmering. Add the mushrooms and cook until they start to brown around the edges, about 5 minutes. Add the garlic and thyme and cook until the garlic is fragrant, about 20 seconds. Season the mushrooms with the salt, pepper, and lemon zest. Continue cooking until the mushrooms are al dente, about 5 more minutes. Remove from the heat and spread the mushrooms on a plate to keep them from overcooking.

Cool the mushrooms to room temperature. Store in an airtight container in the refrigerator for up to 3 days.

LARGE-BATCH OVEN-ROASTED MUSHROOMS

Ingredients

Yield: about 1 quart

1 pound	**cremini mushrooms, stemmed and cut into ¼-inch slices**	454g
1 pound	**shiitake mushrooms, stemmed and cut into ¼-inch slices**	454g
1 pound	**oyster mushrooms, pulled into ¼- to ½-inch strips**	454g
2 teaspoons	**kosher salt, plus more for seasoning**	6g
1 teaspoon	**freshly ground black pepper, plus more for seasoning**	2g
1 or 2 cloves	**garlic, chopped**	5–10g
⅔ cup	**freshly squeezed lemon juice**	160g
¼ cup	**extra-virgin olive oil**	55g
1 sprig each	**fresh thyme, sage, and rosemary, tied together with butcher twine**	10g total

1. Preheat the oven to 400°F. Coat a 9 × 13-inch baking dish with cooking spray.
2. Put the mushrooms in the baking dish. Add the salt, pepper, garlic, lemon juice, and olive oil and toss until the mushrooms are well coated. Add the bundle of herb sprigs.
3. Cover the baking dish with aluminum foil and roast for 1 hour. The mushrooms should be al dente. If they are not, re-cover the baking dish and continue roasting, checking every 10 minutes until done.
4. Drain off two-thirds of the cooking liquid and reserve. Spread the mushrooms and remaining cooking liquid on a rimmed baking sheet and roast for 10 to 15 minutes, until the edges start to brown.
5. Season the mushrooms to taste with more salt and pepper and more cooking liquid as desired.

Cool the mushrooms to room temperature. Store in an airtight container in the refrigerator for up to 3 days.

The lemon juice in this recipe serves two purposes. *First, it adds a delightful lemony flavor to the mushrooms, bringing out the herbiness and earthiness as they cook. Second, it makes the mixture more acidic, an essential step in limiting the chance of botulism growing in dishes that combine mushrooms and/or garlic (or any alliums, like onions or shallots) in oil. Botulism is rare but can occur if these foods are left at room temperature for too long. Even after upping the acidity, it's a good idea to ensure the mixture doesn't spend more than 2 hours at room temperature.*

RATATOUILLE

Yield: about 4 cups

1	**medium zucchini, diced small (about 1 cup)**	130g
1	**medium yellow squash, diced small (about 1 cup)**	130g
2 teaspoons	**kosher salt, divided, plus more to taste**	6g
1	**medium eggplant, diced small (about 2 cups)**	200g
1 cup	**extra-virgin olive oil, divided, plus more as needed**	220g
2 cups	**cherry tomatoes**	250g
	Freshly ground black pepper to taste	
½ cup	**finely chopped Caramelized Onions (page 299)**	140g
2 tablespoons	**Roasted Garlic (page 298)**	25g
2 teaspoons	**chopped fresh basil**	4g
2 teaspoons	**chopped fresh parsley**	4g
1 teaspoon	**chopped fresh tarragon**	1g
½ teaspoon	**chopped fresh thyme**	0.5g
1 tablespoon	**balsamic vinegar, plus more to taste**	13g

1. Place the zucchini and squash in a bowl and toss with 1 teaspoon of the salt.
2. In a separate bowl, toss the eggplant with the remaining 1 teaspoon salt. Let the vegetables stand for 30 minutes.
3. Preheat the oven to 350°F.
4. Drain the diced zucchini and squash and pat dry with paper towels. Place in a 9-inch square baking pan or on a small, rimmed baking sheet, toss with 2 tablespoons of the olive oil, and season to taste with salt and pepper.
5. Rinse the diced eggplant in cold water and pat dry with paper towels. Place in a 9-inch square baking pan or on a small, rimmed baking sheet, toss with 2 tablespoons of the olive oil, and season to taste with salt and pepper.
6. Place the tomatoes in a 9-inch square baking pan or on a small, rimmed baking sheet. Toss with 2 tablespoons of the olive oil and season to taste with salt and pepper.

7 Arrange the vegetables in 1 tight layer in the center of each pan. It's OK if they overlap.

8 Roast until the vegetables are cooked through, but still hold their shape, 20 to 35 minutes. They may brown around the edges. The tomatoes will cook quickest; check for doneness after about 20 minutes. If the eggplant or squash start looking shriveled and dry, add more olive oil and stir the vegetables, then place back in the oven to continue roasting.

9 Let cool, then gently transfer all the vegetables to a large bowl. Fold in the caramelized onions, roasted garlic, herbs, and remaining olive oil. Add a few more teaspoons of olive oil if the mixture seems dry.

10 Add the balsamic vinegar and season to taste with more salt, black pepper, and balsamic vinegar as needed. Cover and chill overnight in the refrigerator to let the flavors develop and blend.

Store in an airtight container in the refrigerator for up to 5 days.

NUT-FREE PESTO

Traditional pesto recipes call for pine nuts, walnuts, or cashews. Here, we use toasted sunflower seeds as a less pricey, nut-free stand-in. (Sunflower seeds are safe for roughly 90 percent of folks with tree nut allergies.) Because we are not using the traditional Parmesan, this pesto is also dairy-free. Feel free to adjust the ratio of herbs based on what you have on hand or what's growing in the garden.

Yield: about 1 cup

1½ cups	**tightly packed fresh basil leaves**	36g
¾ cup	**tightly packed fresh mint leaves**	18g
¼ cup	**chopped fresh chives**	12g
1 tablespoon	**toasted, hulled sunflower seeds**	10g
6 tablespoons	**extra-virgin olive oil**	81g
2 tablespoons	**water or dry white wine**	30g
1½ teaspoons	**kosher salt**	4.5g
1 or 2 cloves	**garlic, roughly chopped**	5–10g

1. Toss together the basil, mint, and chives in a small bowl.
2. Add the olive oil to a blender, followed by the water, sunflower seeds, salt, and garlic. Blend on high speed until roughly combined, about 30 seconds. With the blender running, add the herbs and blend until smooth.

Store the pesto in an airtight container in the refrigerator for up to 5 days. Pesto can be frozen for several months, but why not toss any leftovers with pasta and generous handfuls of freshly grated Parmigiano-Reggiano instead?

If you don't have a blender, you can make the pesto in a food processor. Be sure to scrape down the sides of the bowl between additions.

PESTO MAYO

Make extra for non-biscuit sandwiches too! Pesto mayo is fantastic with sliced deli turkey and chicken, BLTs, grilled cheese, and burgers.

Yield: about ½ cup, or 4 servings

½ cup	**mayonnaise**	115g
1 tablespoon	**Nut-Free Pesto (page 176)**	15g

1 Combine the mayo and pesto in a small bowl and whisk together until well blended.

Store in an airtight container in the refrigerator for up to 5 days.

Angel Biscuits

Angel biscuits use three leavening agents—baking powder, baking soda, and yeast—to achieve their heavenly light texture. The biscuits are a beloved staple in the South, but the recipe's origin is a mystery. Some folks say it was invented in the 1950s by an employee at Martha White or White Lily, competing Nashville-based flour mills. Others say the brands simply popularized an older recipe that dates back to a time when chemical leaveners were finicky and storing fresh yeast was precarious. Using all three in one recipe virtually guarantees a successful bake, and they were often touted as beginner's or bride's biscuits. Today, with stable dried yeast and double-acting baking powder, the biscuits are a revelation. They taste like a cross between an extra-fluffy biscuit and a Parker House roll.

Initially, I punched my angel biscuits out much like I do our buttermilk biscuits, but at some point I began patting them out gently with my hands instead of rolling them with a pin, thinking this might deflate the delicate yeast-risen dough. The results were amazing—tall and crusty on the outside, soft and tender on the inside. This method is the fastest path to a plate of angel biscuits. Then I read country singer Trisha Yearwood's recipe, where she combines her angel biscuit recipe with the Southern technique of folding biscuit dough over onto itself to create rough puff pastry–like layers that spring apart when baked. She bakes hers in a quaint cast-iron skillet. Intrigued, I added as many folds to the biscuits as I could without having to stop and let the dough rest and placed them on a baking sheet. They immediately sprang up in the oven and toppled over. It turns out the cast-iron skillet provides structure, not just homey vibes. The biscuits support each other as they rise, and the interior of the biscuit bakes up even more tender than before. Cast iron holds heat and distributes it evenly without hot spots, so the bottoms of the biscuits crisp up nicely without scorching.

Next page

ANGEL BISCUITS, *continued*

Ingredients

Yield: about 10 (2½- to 3-inch) round biscuits

5 cups	**all-purpose flour**	600g
5 tablespoons	**sugar**	62g
3 tablespoons	**instant yeast**	27g
2 teaspoons	**kosher salt**	6g
1¾ teaspoons	**baking powder**	7g
1 teaspoon	**baking soda**	4g
1 cup (2 sticks)	**cold unsalted butter, grated, plus melted butter for brushing**	227g
¼ cup	**warm water (100 to 110°F)**	57g
2 cups	**buttermilk**	454g

1. In a medium to large bowl, combine the flour, sugar, yeast, salt, baking powder, and baking soda (you need lots of extra room to knead the dough). Add the grated butter and mix it into the flour mixture until it resembles a coarse meal.
2. Make a well in the center and add the warm water and buttermilk. Stir with a wooden spoon or silicone spatula or mix with your hands until it forms a loose ball. Knead the dough together a few times in the bowl just to incorporate all the flour.
3. Turn the dough out onto a floured work surface and knead for 10 to 12 minutes, until smooth. Return the dough to the bowl and cover it with plastic wrap or a clean dish towel. Place the bowl in a warm spot to rise until roughly double in size, about 1 hour.
4. Preheat the oven to 425°F.
5. Transfer the dough to a lightly floured work surface and gently press it into a 1-inch-thick rectangle. Do not use a rolling pin—it will deflate the dough.
6. Gently fold the dough by lifting the right edge and aligning it with the left edge. Press the dough back down into a 1-inch-thick rectangle. Next, fold the dough toward you, aligning the top and bottom edges. Pat into a 1-inch-thick rectangle. Then, fold the left edge of the dough to meet the right edge of the dough. Gently pat the dough back into a 1-inch-thick rectangle. (The dough may start to fight you at this point. Be patient and keep gently patting the dough.) Finally, fold the bottom edge of the dough up to meet the top edge of the dough. Pat into a 1- to 1½-inch-thick rectangle.
7. Punch out the biscuits using a 2½- to 3-inch round biscuit or cookie cutter, dipping the cutter in flour between each biscuit. Gather the dough scraps, knead them together, and roll again. Punch out the remaining biscuits.

8 Brush an 11-inch cast-iron skillet with melted butter.

9 Arrange the biscuits in the skillet, starting with the outside edge, and brush with melted butter.

10 Bake for 15 to 20 minutes, until the tops and bottoms of the biscuits are a deep caramel color. Brush the warm biscuits with melted butter and serve immediately.

Angel biscuits are best eaten right out of the oven. Store any leftovers in an airtight container at room temperature overnight and toast before serving.

Saffron Angel Biscuits

Make angel biscuits even more heavenly by infusing saffron into the dough. Saffron has a subtle floral, honey-like sweetness and a lovely yellow hue that works well with this delicate biscuit. Only a pinch of the bright red threads is needed, which is fortunate since saffron is the world's most expensive spice. Even so, you might want to make sure you've mastered the original angel biscuit recipe before trying this variation. Be warned, saffron was used to dye royal robes in ancient times, and it will do the same for your clean white apron!

Ingredients

Yield: about 10 (2½- to 3-inch) round biscuits

2 cups	**buttermilk**	454g
¼ teaspoon	**saffron threads**	~0.2g
5 cups	**all-purpose flour**	600g
5 tablespoons	**sugar**	62g
3 tablespoons	**instant yeast**	27g
2 teaspoons	**kosher salt**	6g
1¾ teaspoons	**baking powder**	7g
1 teaspoon	**baking soda**	4g
1 cup (2 sticks)	**cold unsalted butter, grated, plus melted butter for brushing**	227g
¼ cup	**warm water (100 to 110°F)**	57g

1 In a small, heavy-bottomed saucepan, combine the buttermilk and saffron threads. Heat gently over medium heat, stirring frequently, until the saffron threads start to release color. Do not let the buttermilk boil. Remove the pan from the heat, cover, and let the saffron steep for 15 to 20 minutes. Pour the buttermilk through a fine-mesh sieve into a bowl or glass measuring cup. Push any curds that are separated in the buttermilk through the sieve.

Next page

SAFFRON ANGEL BISCUITS, *continued*

2 In a medium to large bowl, combine the flour, sugar, yeast, salt, baking powder, and baking soda (you need lots of extra room to knead the dough). Add the grated butter and mix it into the flour mixture until it resembles a coarse meal. Make a well in the center and add the warm water and saffron-infused buttermilk. Stir with a wooden spoon or silicone spatula or mix with your hands until it forms a loose ball. Knead the dough together a few times in the bowl just to incorporate all the flour.

3 Turn the dough out onto a floured work surface and knead for 10 to 12 minutes, until smooth. Return the dough to the bowl and cover it with plastic wrap or a clean dish towel. Place the bowl in a warm spot to rise until roughly double in size, about 1 hour.

4 Preheat the oven to 425°F.

5 Transfer the dough to a lightly floured work surface and gently press it into a 1-inch-thick rectangle. Do not use a rolling pin—it will deflate the dough. Gently fold the dough by lifting the right edge and aligning it with the left edge. Press the dough back down into a 1-inch-thick rectangle. Next, fold the dough toward you, aligning the top and bottom edges. Pat into a 1-inch-thick rectangle. Then, fold the left edge of the dough to meet the right edge of the dough. Gently pat the dough back into a 1-inch-thick rectangle. (The dough may start to fight you at this point. Be patient and keep gently patting the dough.) Finally, fold the bottom edge of the dough up to meet the top edge of the dough. Pat into a 1- to 1½-inch-thick rectangle.

6 Punch out the biscuits using a 2½- to 3-inch round biscuit or cookie cutter, dipping the cutter in flour between each biscuit. Gather the dough scraps, knead them together, and roll again. Punch out the remaining biscuits. Brush an 11-inch cast-iron skillet with melted butter. Arrange the biscuits in the skillet, starting with the outside edge, and brush with melted butter. Bake for 15 to 20 minutes, until the tops and bottoms of the biscuits are a deep caramel color. Brush the warm biscuits with melted butter and serve immediately.

Angel biscuits are best eaten right out of the oven. Store any leftovers in an airtight container at room temperature overnight and toast before serving.

Drop Biscuits

Drop biscuits are sometimes called emergency biscuits, and it's easy to see why. They are quick and simple to throw together—the shortest distance between you and a plate of hot biscuits. The loose batter is dropped directly from a spoon onto a baking sheet, so no kneading is required. Grate the butter directly into the dry ingredients to make mixing even faster. They're perfect when you need a quick side with dinner, a vehicle for homemade jam, a last-minute base for biscuits and gravy, or anytime a biscuit would lift your spirits on a trying day.

Ingredients

Yield: about 10 biscuits

2 cups	**all-purpose flour**	240g
1 teaspoon	**sugar**	4g
1 tablespoon	**baking powder**	12g
¾ teaspoon	**kosher salt**	2.25g
½ teaspoon	**baking soda**	2g
½ cup (1 stick) plus 2 tablespoons	**cold unsalted butter**	141g
¾ cup	**buttermilk**	170g

1 Preheat the oven to 425°F.

2 In a medium bowl, whisk together the flour, sugar, baking powder, salt, and baking soda. Grate the butter using the shredder side of a box grater (the wide side with ¼-inch holes). Toss the grated butter in the dry ingredients to incorporate. Work the butter into the flour mixture with your fingers until it resembles a coarse meal.

3 Make a well in the center and pour in the buttermilk. Mix the dough in the bowl by hand until smooth. It will be sticky.

Next page

DROP BISCUITS, *continued*

4 Stack one rimmed baking sheet on top of another and line with parchment paper or coat with cooking spray. (The double panning keeps the bottoms of the biscuits from overbrowning. This may not be necessary if you have an insulated or extra-heavy baking sheet.) Using a ⅓-cup measure, drop the dough 2 inches apart on the baking sheet.

5 Bake for 15 minutes, or until the body of each biscuit is golden and the spiky top edges are dark golden brown. The biscuits will sound hollow when tapped on the bottom. Serve immediately.

Drop biscuits taste best fresh from the oven. They lose their delightful crispiness if they sit too long. Store any leftovers in an airtight container at room temperature overnight and toast in a toaster or 350°F oven.

Grating and working the butter into the dough by hand brings these biscuits together in minutes and cuts down on cleanup, making them an excellent choice for a busy day. Make sure your butter is very cold before you grate it, and watch your fingers!

Bacon Fat & Collard Green Drop Biscuits

Bacon fat gives these biscuits a wonderful smoky flavor and extra-flaky texture. If you have time, cook the greens a day or two ahead. The collards get more tender and less bitter, and soak up more bacon and garlic flavor as they sit.

Ingredients

Yield: about 12 biscuits

2 cups	**all-purpose flour**	240g
1 tablespoon	**baking powder**	12g
1 teaspoon	**sugar**	4g
¾ teaspoon	**kosher salt**	2.25g
½ teaspoon	**smoked paprika**	1.2g
½ teaspoon	**baking soda**	2g
¼ cup (½ stick)	**cold unsalted butter**	57g
6 tablespoons	**bacon fat, frozen**	78g
½ cup	**Sautéed Collard Greens (page 297)**	~120g
¾ cup	**buttermilk**	170g

1 Preheat the oven to 425°F.

2 In a medium bowl, whisk together the flour, baking powder, sugar, salt, smoked paprika, and baking soda. Grate the butter using the shredder side of a box grater (the wide side with ¼-inch holes). Toss the bacon fat and grated butter in the dry ingredients to incorporate. Work the fats into the flour mixture with your fingers until the mixture looks shaggy. Add the collard greens and continue working the greens and fats into the flour mixture until it resembles a coarse meal.

3 Make a well in the center and pour in the buttermilk. Mix the dough gently by hand until it just comes together.

4 Stack one rimmed baking sheet on top of another and line with parchment paper or coat with cooking spray. (The double panning keeps the bottoms of the biscuits from overbrowning. This may not be necessary if you have an insulated or extra-heavy baking sheet.) Using a ¼-cup scoop, drop the dough 1 inch apart on the baking sheet.

5 Bake for 15 to 16 minutes, until the biscuits' tops and bottoms are dark golden brown. When tapped on the bottom, the biscuits will sound hollow. Serve immediately.

Drop biscuits taste best fresh from the oven. They lose their delightful crispiness if they sit too long. Store any leftovers in an airtight container at room temperature overnight and retoast in a 350°F oven.

Heirloom Tomato & Parmesan Drop Biscuits

These biscuits are full of nutty, buttery Parmesan flavor and pops of heirloom tomato sweetness. Bonus: They come together in minutes. Be sure to seek out heirloom tomatoes from a farmers' market or, if you are lucky, your own garden. They are sweeter, meatier, and thinner-skinned than commercially grown varieties.

Ingredients

Yield: 6 to 8 biscuits

1	**medium heirloom tomato**	150g
2 cups	**all-purpose flour**	240g
4 teaspoons	**baking powder**	16g
1 tablespoon	**sugar**	12g
1 teaspoon	**kosher salt**	3g
½ teaspoon	**freshly ground black pepper**	1g
¼ cup	**grated or shredded Parmesan cheese**	25g
½ cup (1 stick) plus 2 tablespoons	**cold unsalted butter**	141g
½ cup	**whole milk**	120g

1 Preheat the oven to 425°F.

2 Peel (see sidebar), core, and chop the tomato into roughly ½-inch cubes; you should have about 1 cup. Set aside on a paper towel to soak up excess moisture.

3 In a medium bowl, whisk together the flour, baking powder, sugar, salt, and pepper. Add the Parmesan cheese. Grate the butter using the shredder side of a box grater (the wide side with ¼-inch holes). Toss the grated butter in the dry ingredients to incorporate. Work the butter into the flour mixture with your fingers until the mixture resembles a coarse meal. Toss the tomato cubes in the flour mixture to coat with flour.

Next page

HEIRLOOM TOMATO & PARMESAN DROP BISCUITS, *continued*

4 Make a well in the center and pour in the milk. Mix the dough gently by hand in the bowl until it just comes together.

5 Stack one rimmed baking sheet on top of another and line with parchment paper or coat with cooking spray. (The double panning keeps the bottoms of the biscuits from overbrowning. This may not be necessary if you have an insulated or extra-heavy baking sheet.) Using a ⅓-cup measure, drop the dough 2 inches apart on the baking sheet.

6 Bake for 20 to 25 minutes, until the tops and bottoms of the biscuits are dark golden brown. The biscuits will sound hollow when tapped on the bottom. Use a spatula to gently lift the biscuits off the baking sheet. The tomato chunks will stick to the baking sheet and the biscuits can break if lifted off by hand. Serve immediately.

Drop biscuits taste best fresh from the oven. They lose their delightful crispiness if they sit too long. Store any leftovers in an airtight container at room temperature overnight and retoast in a 350°F oven.

PEELING TOMATOES

Heirloom tomatoes are easy to peel because of their thin skin and dense flesh. If you are making the standard-size recipe, peeling a tomato with a reasonably sharp paring knife will take little time. For bigger batches, the same blanching method we use for peaches and other stone fruit works well for tomatoes too. Fill a mixing bowl halfway with ice water. Bring a pot of water to a boil on the stove. Cut an X on the bottom of the fruit and drop it in the boiling water for 10 to 20 seconds. Transfer the fruit one by one to the bowl of ice water. After a few seconds, the skin should separate from the flesh. Usually, if the tomato or peach is ripe, you can pull the skin off in strips by hand. Sometimes you need to use a paring knife to grab the skin at the top of the fruit and coax it away from the flesh. For particularly stubborn cases, place the fruit in the boiling water for 10 more seconds and repeat the process. Just be careful not to let it cook!

Peach Drop Biscuits

This is a great recipe for anytime you have especially juicy peaches. We use the extra juice to flavor the dough and to make a fresh peach glaze to drizzle on top. If you don't have quite enough juice, you can substitute store-bought peach juice, peach nectar, or water for the biscuits and store-bought juice, nectar, or whole milk for the glaze. It was inspired by Jerrelle Guy's Strawberry Drop Biscuits recipe in the *New York Times*. Make sure to let the peaches sit and dry out a bit before you mix up the biscuits.

Ingredients

Yield: 6 to 8 biscuits

¾ cup	**peaches (about 1 large peach)**	150g
1½ cups plus 2 tablespoons	**all-purpose flour, divided**	190g
¼ cup	**granulated sugar**	50g
4 teaspoons	**baking powder**	16g
½ teaspoon	**kosher salt**	1.5g
½ cup plus 2 tablespoons	**cold unsalted butter**	141g
¼ cup	**heavy cream**	60g
¼ teaspoon	**almond extract (optional)**	1g
1 cup	**powdered sugar**	120g
1 tablespoon	**whole milk**	15g

1. Peel (see page 192), pit, and chop the peach into roughly ½-inch cubes; you should have about ¾ cup. Cover and set aside for 1 hour at room temperature or overnight in the refrigerator. Drain the peaches. Measure out 5 tablespoons juice and reserve.

2. Preheat the oven to 425°F.

Next page

PEACH DROP BISCUITS, *continued*

3 In a medium bowl, whisk together 1½ cups of the flour, granulated sugar, baking powder, and salt. Grate the butter using the shredder side of a box grater (the wide side with ¼-inch holes). Toss the grated butter in the dry ingredients to incorporate. Work the butter into the flour mixture with your fingers until the mixture resembles a coarse meal. Toss the peaches in the remaining 2 tablespoons flour and add them to the flour mixture.

4 Make a well in the center and pour in the heavy cream, 4 tablespoons of the reserved peach juice, and the optional almond extract. Mix the dough gently by hand in the bowl until it just comes together.

5 Stack one rimmed baking sheet on top of another and line with parchment paper or coat with cooking spray. (The double panning keeps the bottoms of the biscuits from overbrowning. This may not be necessary if you have an insulated or extra-heavy baking sheet.) Using a ⅓-cup measure, drop the dough 2 inches apart on the baking sheet.

6 Bake for 20 to 25 minutes, until the tops and bottoms of the biscuits are dark golden brown. The biscuits will sound hollow when tapped on the bottom. Use a spatula to gently lift the biscuits off the baking sheet. The peach chunks may stick to the baking sheet and the biscuits can break if lifted off by hand. Let cool to room temperature.

7 In a small bowl with tall sides, combine the powdered sugar and remaining 1 tablespoon peach juice and mix to form a smooth paste, then add the milk and mix until smooth. Drizzle the glaze over the cooled biscuits with a fork or whisk.

Drop biscuits taste best just after they have been cooled and glazed. They lose their delightful crispiness if they sit too long. Store any leftovers in an airtight container at room temperature overnight and retoast in a 350°F oven.

PEACHES
$9 2 for $16

Rosemary, Black Pepper & Gruyère Drop Biscuits

Adding fresh herbs and a flavorful cheese is an easy way to dress up a simple drop biscuit. This flavor combination is one of my favorites, but feel free to swap in other herbs and cheeses, depending on what you have on hand. It's a great way to use up leftover ingredients from other recipes.

Yield: about 10 biscuits

Amount	Ingredient	Weight
2 cups	**all-purpose flour**	240g
1 tablespoon	**baking powder**	12g
1 teaspoon	**sugar**	4g
1 teaspoon	**kosher salt**	3g
1 teaspoon	**freshly ground black pepper, plus more for finishing**	2g
½ teaspoon	**baking soda**	2g
5 tablespoons	**finely chopped fresh rosemary**	7.5g
¾ cup	**shredded Gruyère cheese**	85g
½ cup (1 stick) plus 2 tablespoons	**cold unsalted butter, plus melted butter for brushing**	141g
¾ cup	**buttermilk**	170g

1 Preheat the oven to 425°F.

2 In a medium bowl, whisk together the flour, baking powder, sugar, salt, pepper, baking soda, and rosemary. Add the Gruyère and toss to incorporate. Grate the butter using the shredder side of a box grater (the wide side with ¼-inch holes). Toss the grated butter in the dry ingredients to incorporate. Work the butter into the flour mixture with your fingers until it resembles a coarse meal.

3 Make a well in the center and pour in the buttermilk. Mix the dough by hand in the bowl until smooth. It will be sticky.

4 Stack one rimmed baking sheet on top of another and line with parchment paper or coat with cooking spray. (The double panning keeps the bottoms of the biscuits from overbrowning. This may not be necessary if you have an insulated or extra-heavy baking sheet.) Using a ⅓-cup measure, drop the dough 2 inches apart on the baking sheet.

5 Bake for 15 minutes, or until the body of each biscuit is golden and the spiky top edges are dark golden brown. The biscuits will sound hollow when tapped on the bottom.

6 Brush the warm biscuits with melted butter and top with freshly ground black pepper; serve immediately.

Drop biscuits taste best fresh from the oven. They lose their delightful crispiness if they sit too long. Store any leftovers in an airtight container at room temperature overnight and retoast in a 350°F oven.

Red Cornmeal Drop Biscuits

This is a quick and easy favorite with lots of texture. Serve it in the morning with a spoonful of blueberry jam or at suppertime with hearty soups and chili. I like to use stone-ground cornmeal, specifically the red heirloom Bloody Butcher variety, for extra crunch, but blue and yellow cornmeal varieties are tasty, too. Choose a medium- or fine-grind cornmeal if you prefer a more delicate crumb.

Ingredients

Yield: 6 to 8 biscuits

2 cups	**all-purpose flour**	240g
⅔ cup	**cornmeal**	92g
1 tablespoon	**baking powder**	12g
2 teaspoons	**kosher salt**	6g
½ teaspoon	**baking soda**	2g
½ teaspoon	**sugar**	2g
¼ teaspoon	**freshly ground black pepper**	0.6g
1¼ cups (2½ sticks)	**cold unsalted butter**	284g
1¼ cups	**buttermilk**	284g

1. Preheat the oven to 425°F.
2. In a medium bowl, whisk together the flour, cornmeal, baking powder, salt, baking soda, sugar, and black pepper. Grate the butter using the shredder side of a box grater (the wide side with ¼-inch holes). Toss the grated butter in the dry ingredients to incorporate. Work the butter into the flour mixture with your fingers until it resembles a coarse meal.
3. Make a well in the center and pour in the buttermilk. Mix the dough gently by hand in the bowl until it just comes together.

4 Stack one rimmed baking sheet on top of another and line with parchment paper or coat with cooking spray. (The double panning keeps the bottoms of the biscuits from overbrowning. This may not be necessary if you have an insulated or extra-heavy baking sheet.) Using a ⅓-cup measure, drop the dough 2 inches apart on the baking sheet.

5 Bake for 20 to 25 minutes, until the tops and bottoms of the biscuits are dark golden brown. The biscuits will sound hollow when tapped on the bottom. Serve immediately.

Drop biscuits taste best fresh from the oven. They lose their delightful crispiness if they sit too long. Store any leftovers in an airtight container at room temperature overnight and retoast in a 350°F oven.

CHAPTER 4

Quick Breads

At its broadest definition, a quick bread is any baked good that uses a chemical leavener like baking soda instead of yeast. You don't have to wait for the yeast to proof, so it is a quick bread. Biscuits, muffins, scones, cakes, brownies, and even pancakes are all technically quick breads. But, for our purposes, quick breads are any bready pastry that tastes better in loaf form or, let's face it, that we like to bake in cute little pans. There is something so homey and delightful about that self-contained shape.

I am lucky to have a colleague who bakes hundreds of mini pumpkin loaves to send as gifts during the holidays. My kids know to watch for the package now and I haven't gotten a slice in two years! Would they get that excited about a muffin? Unlikely.

Loaf pans come in a multitude of shapes and sizes. The closest thing to a standard size is 8½ × 4½ inches, which is sometimes referred to as a 1-pound loaf pan. However, 9 × 5-inch and 8 × 4-inch pans are also common. Your best bet is to take some measurements. Measure across the top of the pan, which is usually slightly bigger than the bottom of the pan.

Recipes in this section are scaled to make one 8½ × 4½-inch loaf, four 5¾ × 3-inch quarter loaves, or eight 3⅞ × 2½-inch mini loaves. When in doubt, fill the pan two-thirds full with batter and keep a close eye on it while it bakes. Quick breads are done when a toothpick inserted in the middle of the loaf comes out clean.

Browned Butter Banana-Nutella Bread

These mini loaves are a staple at the pie shop, where they are known to mysteriously disappear from the cooling rack from time to time. Be sure to brown the butter before you measure it and include any bits of browned butter scraped up from the bottom of the pan.

Ingredients

Yield: 8 mini loaves or 4 quarter loaves or 1 standard loaf

½ cup	**Browned Butter (page 293)**	113g
3	**medium ripe bananas, peeled and mashed**	340–400g
¼ cup	**sugar**	50g
¼ cup	**sour cream**	60g
2	**large eggs**	100g
1 tablespoon	**honey**	21g
1 teaspoon	**vanilla paste**	5g
2 cups	**all-purpose flour**	240g
1 teaspoon	**baking soda**	4g
¼ teaspoon	**kosher salt**	0.75g
¼ cup	**Nutella**	74g

1 Preheat the oven to 350°F. Prepare 8 mini loaf pans, 4 quarter loaf pans, or 1 standard loaf pan by greasing or lining with parchment paper.

2 In a large bowl, combine the browned butter, bananas, sugar, sour cream, eggs, honey, and vanilla paste. Mix with a silicone spatula or wooden spoon until the ingredients are well combined and the bananas are broken up. If you like a chunkier texture, you can leave some larger pieces of banana.

3 In a small bowl, whisk together the flour, baking soda, and salt. Fold flour mixture into the banana mixture until there are no streaks of flour. Be careful not to overmix.

4 For each mini loaf, scoop ¾ cup batter into each pan, top with 1 tablespoon of Nutella, and swirl into the batter with a small offset spatula or butter knife. For each quarter loaf, scoop 1½ cups batter into each pan, top with 2 tablespoons Nutella, and swirl into the batter with a small offset spatula or butter knife. For a standard loaf, scoop half of the batter into the pan and top with half the Nutella, swirling it into the batter with a small offset spatula or a butter knife. Top with the remaining batter and swirl the remaining Nutella into the top of the loaf.

5 Bake for 20 to 25 minutes for mini loaves, 30 to 35 minutes for quarter loaves, and about 1 hour for a standard loaf, or until a cake tester inserted in the middle of the loaf comes out clean.

The honey and the mashed bananas keep the bread extra moist so it can be made ahead and frozen for up to 2 weeks. Thaw it wrapped at room temperature for about 3 hours. Store well-wrapped baked loaves at room temperature for up to 2 days.

PREP NOTE

Do not overmix.

Toffee Banana Bread Variation

Bananas and toffee are a fantastic combination—something we discovered trying to "use up" leftover toffee garnishes we make for pies. I debated including a toffee recipe here since it seems like a lot of extra effort in a section with "quick" in the title, but bananas and sesame seeds together are such an unexpected treat that I did it anyway. If you don't feel like making your own toffee, substitute an equal amount of chopped store-bought toffee, like Skor or Heath bars.

Ingredients

Yield: 8 mini loaves or 4 quarter loaves or 1 standard loaf

1 recipe	**Browned Butter Banana-Nutella Bread batter (page 206)**
¾ cup plus 2 tablespoons	**Sesame Toffee (recipe follows), chopped**

1. Preheat the oven to 350°F. Prepare 8 mini loaf pans, 4 quarter loaf pans, or 1 standard loaf pan by greasing or lining with parchment paper.
2. Make the banana bread batter according to the Browned Butter Banana-Nutella Bread recipe (page 206).
3. Roughly chop the sesame toffee and measure out ¾ cup plus 2 tablespoons.
4. For mini loaves, fill each prepared mini loaf pan with ⅓ cup batter. Scatter 2 teaspoons of toffee over the batter. Spread another ⅓ cup batter over the toffee in each pan, and smooth with an offset spatula or the back of a spoon. Scatter 1 tablespoon of toffee on top of each loaf, pressing it gently into the batter.
5. For quarter loaves, fill each prepared loaf pan with ¾ cup batter. Divide half of the toffee among the four pans. Spread ¾ cup batter over the toffee in each pan. Smooth with an offset spatula or the back of a spoon. Scatter the remaining toffee on top, pressing it gently into the batter.

6 For a standard loaf, transfer half of the batter to the prepared loaf pan. Scatter half of the toffee over the batter. Spread the rest of the batter on top. Smooth with an offset spatula or the back of a spoon. Scatter the remaining toffee on top, pressing it gently into the batter

7 Bake for 20 to 25 minutes (mini loaves), 30 to 35 minutes (quarter loaves), or 1 hour (standard loaf), until a cake tester comes out clean.

Store loaves, well wrapped, at room temperature for up to 2 days or in the freezer for up to 2 weeks.

SESAME TOFFEE

1 cup	**sugar**	198g
6 tablespoons	**water**	85g
7 tablespoons plus 1 teaspoon	**corn syrup**	143g
¾ cup plus 2 tablespoons	**sesame seeds**	125g
1½ teaspoons	**kosher salt**	9g
1 tablespoon	**unsalted butter**	15g
1½ teaspoons	**vanilla paste**	7g
1½ teaspoons	**baking soda**	3g

1 Line a 9⅝ × 13-inch rimmed baking sheet with parchment paper and coat with cooking spray.

2 Combine the sugar and water in a medium, heavy-bottomed saucepan.

3 Add the corn syrup and cook to 240°F.

4 Add the sesame seeds and bring to 311°F.

5 Add the salt and butter.

6 Remove from the heat and quickly stir in the vanilla paste and baking soda.

7 Immediately spread onto the prepared baking sheet. Store in a cool, dry space until toffee sets.

Store in an airtight container at room temperature for up to 1 week.

Chocolate Pound Cake

This is a chocolate pound cake for the big kids. It is rich, moist, and not too sweet, with a hint of crème de cacao. I developed this recipe for a fine-dining restaurant, where we used tiny slices as the base for elaborate desserts. Now I simply eat it plain with a cup of coffee (delicious!).

Ingredients

Yield: 8 mini loaves or 4 quarter loaves or 1 standard loaf

5	**large eggs**	250g
1 cup (2 sticks)	**unsalted butter, softened to room temperature**	227g
1¾ cups	**sugar**	350g
5 ounces (heaping ¾ cup)	**semisweet chocolate chips, melted**	142g
1 tablespoon	**crème de cacao**	15g
1½ cups	**all-purpose flour**	180g
½ cup	**cocoa powder, preferably Dutch-processed**	43g
¼ teaspoon	**kosher salt**	0.75g

1. Preheat the oven to 350°F. Prepare 8 mini loaf pans, 4 quarter loaf pans, or 1 standard loaf pan by greasing or lining with parchment paper.
2. To warm the eggs, fill a bowl with room-temperature water and add the eggs. Set aside for 20 minutes, then drain the bowl and dry off the eggs.
3. Using a hand mixer or a stand mixer, cream the butter until light and fluffy. Slowly add the sugar, scraping down the sides as needed. Continue to mix until the sugar is completely incorporated. Add the eggs one at a time, mixing to incorporate completely. Fold in the melted chocolate chips and crème de cacao. Sift in the flour, cocoa powder, and salt until just combined.
4. Scoop ½ cup batter into each mini loaf pan, 1 cup batter into each quarter loaf pan, or all the batter into a standard loaf pan. Bake for 20 to 25 minutes (mini loaves), 30 to 35 minutes (quarter loaves), or 1 hour (standard loaf), until a cake tester comes out clean.

Store loaves, well wrapped, at room temperature for up to 2 days or in the freezer for up to 2 weeks.

Coffee-Date Pound Cake

My assistant pastry chef Kim Brown developed this recipe one January when I was bemoaning the lack of fresh fruit for pastries and missing the summery crème fraîche pound cakes. The combination of rich, sweet dates, sharp coffee, caramelly brown sugar, and rum is guaranteed to make you feel cozy and pampered on even the dreariest winter day.

Ingredients

Yield: 8 mini loaves or 4 quarter loaves or 1 standard loaf

1⅓ cups	**pitted dates**	200g
	Hot brewed coffee or espresso, enough to cover dates	
7 tablespoons	**unsalted butter, softened to room temperature**	99g
1 cup	**packed light brown sugar**	213g
3	**large eggs**	150g
½ teaspoon	**vanilla paste**	2.5g
1¾ cups	**all-purpose flour**	210g
¾ teaspoon	**baking powder**	3g
1 teaspoon	**baking soda**	4g
½ teaspoon	**kosher salt**	1.5g
1 recipe	**Simple Glaze or Espresso Glaze (page 291), for finishing (optional)**	

1 Preheat the oven to 350°F. Prepare 8 mini loaf pans, 4 quarter loaf pans, or 1 standard loaf pan by greasing or lining with parchment paper.

2 Roughly chop the dates and put them in a heatproof bowl. Pour in enough hot coffee or espresso to cover them. Let stand for 20 to 60 minutes, then pour off any coffee that wasn't absorbed.

3 Using a hand mixer or a stand mixer, cream the butter and brown sugar until light and fluffy. Add the eggs, one at a time, scraping down the bowl after each addition. Add the vanilla paste, mixing to incorporate completely. Sift together the flour, baking powder, baking soda, and salt and fold into the batter until just a few streaks of flour remain. Add the dates, then fold to incorporate until just combined.

4 Scoop ½ cup batter into each mini loaf pan, 1 cup batter into each quarter loaf pan, or all the batter into a standard loaf pan. Bake for 20 to 25 minutes (mini loaves), 30 to 35 minutes (quarter loaves), or 1 hour (standard loaf), until a cake tester comes out clean. Set aside to cool completely, then ice the cakes with simple glaze or espresso glaze, if using.

Store loaves, well wrapped, at room temperature for up to 3 days or in the freezer for up to 2 weeks.

Crème Fraîche Loaf

This is a lovely, light, cake-like loaf. Former assistant pastry chef Kasey Pillow developed it for rhubarb season, but we have added all kinds of fruit over the years and it is always delightful. For finishing, a light dusting of powdered sugar in place of the glazes does just fine.

Ingredients

Yield: 8 mini loaves or 4 quarter loaves or 1 standard loaf

1 cup	**sugar**	200g
3	**large eggs**	150g
1 cup	**crème fraîche**	240g
2¼ cups	**all-purpose flour**	270g
1 tablespoon	**baking powder**	12g
Pinch	**kosher salt**	
	Grated zest of 1 lemon	
½ teaspoon	**vanilla paste**	2.5g
1 recipe	**Simple Glaze or variation (page 291), for finishing (optional)**	

1. Preheat the oven to 350°F. Prepare 8 mini loaf pans, 4 quarter loaf pans, or 1 standard loaf pan by greasing or lining with parchment paper.
2. In a large bowl, whisk together the sugar and eggs until the mixture is pale and thickened. Add the crème fraîche and mix well to incorporate.
3. Whisk together the flour, baking powder, and salt and fold into the batter. Gently fold in the lemon zest and vanilla paste.
4. Scoop ½ cup batter into each mini loaf pan, 1 cup batter into each quarter loaf pan, or all the batter into a standard loaf pan. Bake for 20 to 25 minutes (mini loaves), 30 to 35 minutes (quarter loaves), or 1 hour (standard loaf), until a cake tester comes out clean. Set aside to cool completely, then ice the cakes with simple glaze, if using.

Store loaves, well wrapped, at room temperature for up to 2 days or in the freezer for up to 2 weeks.

Cranberry Loaf

Ingredients

Yield: 8 mini loaves or 4 quarter loaves or 1 standard loaf

1 cup	**granulated sugar**	200g
3	**large eggs**	150g
1 cup	**crème fraîche**	240g
2¼ cups	**all-purpose flour**	270g
1 tablespoon	**baking powder**	12g
Pinch	**kosher salt**	
	Grated zest of 1 orange	
½ teaspoon	**vanilla paste**	2.5g
1 cup	**fresh cranberries, halved**	100g
1 recipe	**Orange Glaze (page 291), for finishing (optional)**	

1 Preheat the oven to 350°F. Prepare 8 mini loaf pans, 4 quarter loaf pans, or 1 standard loaf pan by greasing or lining with parchment paper.

2 In a large bowl, whisk together the sugar and eggs until the mixture is pale and ribboned. Add the crème fraîche and mix well to incorporate. Whisk together the flour, baking powder, and salt and fold into the batter. Gently fold in the orange zest and vanilla paste.

3 For each mini loaf, scoop 2 tablespoons batter into each pan, top with 2 tablespoons cranberries, then another 2 tablespoons batter. For each quarter loaf, scoop ¼ cup batter into each pan, top with ¼ cup cranberries, then another ¼ cup batter. For a standard loaf, scoop half of the batter into the pan, top with all the cranberries, then the remaining batter.

4 Bake for 20 to 25 minutes (mini loaves), 30 to 35 minutes (quarter loaves), or 1 hour (standard loaf), until a cake tester comes out clean. Set aside to cool completely, then ice with orange glaze, if using.

Store loaves, well wrapped, at room temperature for up to 2 days or in the freezer for up to 2 weeks.

Gooseberry Loaf

Gooseberry bushes have long, sharp thorns that keep birds and most people from eating the berries, which is too bad because they make lovely pies and pastries. They taste like tart grapes and turn wonderfully jammy when cooked. Gooseberry season runs from May through August. The berries start out green and turn a deep purple when fully ripe later in the season. Since they must be hand-picked, your best bet is to find them at your local farmers' market.

Ingredients

Yield: 8 mini loaves or 4 quarter loaves or 1 standard loaf

1 cup	**granulated sugar**	200g
3	**large eggs**	150g
1 cup	**crème fraîche**	240g
2¼ cups	**all-purpose flour**	270g
1 tablespoon	**baking powder**	12g
Pinch	**kosher salt**	
	Grated zest of 1 lemon	
½ teaspoon	**vanilla paste**	2.5g
1 cup	**fresh or frozen whole gooseberries**	140g
	Powdered sugar, for finishing (optional)	

1 Preheat the oven to 350°F. Prepare 8 mini loaf pans, 4 quarter loaf pans, or 1 standard loaf pan by greasing or lining with parchment paper.

2 In a large bowl, whisk together the granulated sugar and eggs until the mixture is pale and thickened. Add the crème fraîche and mix well to incorporate. Whisk together the flour, baking powder, and salt and fold into the batter. Gently fold in the lemon zest and vanilla paste.

3 For each mini loaf, scoop 2 tablespoons batter into each pan, top with 2 tablespoons gooseberries, then another 2 tablespoons batter. For each quarter loaf, scoop ¼ cup batter into each pan, top with ¼ cup gooseberries, then another ¼ cup batter. For a standard loaf, scoop half of the batter into the pan, top with all the gooseberries, then the remaining batter.

4 Bake for 20 to 25 minutes (mini loaves), 30 to 35 minutes (quarter loaves), or 1 hour (standard loaf), until a cake tester comes out clean. Set aside to cool, then dust with powdered sugar, if using.

Store loaves, well wrapped, at room temperature for up to 2 days or in the freezer for up to 2 weeks.

Peach Basil Loaf

Peach and basil is one of my favorite flavor combinations. If you are lucky enough to find cinnamon basil at your local farmers' market, snatch it up. The extra hint of cinnamon makes it even better.

Ingredients

Yield: 8 mini loaves or 4 quarter loaves or 1 standard loaf

1 cup	**sugar**	200g
3	**large eggs**	150g
1 cup	**crème fraîche**	240g
2¼ cups plus 1 tablespoon	**all-purpose flour, divided**	275g
1 tablespoon	**baking powder**	12g
	Grated zest of 1 lemon	
½ teaspoon	**vanilla paste**	2.5g
Pinch	**kosher salt**	
2 tablespoons	**thinly sliced fresh basil, divided**	4g
1 tablespoon	**peach juice**	15g
1 cup	**peaches, peeled (instructions on page 192), pitted, and cut into 1-inch pieces**	150g
1 recipe	**Peach Glaze (page 291), for finishing (optional)**	

1 Preheat the oven to 350°F. Prepare 8 mini loaf pans, 4 quarter loaf pans, or 1 standard loaf pan by greasing or lining with parchment paper.

2 In a large bowl, whisk together the sugar and eggs until the mixture is pale and ribboned. Add the crème fraîche and mix well to incorporate. Combine 2¼ cups of the flour and the baking powder and fold into the batter. Add the lemon zest, vanilla paste, salt, 1 tablespoon of the basil, and the peach juice and fold just to incorporate.

3 Toss the peaches with the remaining 1 tablespoon flour to coat.

4 For each mini loaf, scoop 2 tablespoons batter into each pan, top with 2 tablespoons peaches, then another 2 tablespoons batter. For each quarter loaf, scoop ¼ cup batter into each pan, then ¼ cup peaches, then another ¼ cup batter. For a standard loaf, scoop half of the batter into the pan, then all the peaches, then the remaining batter.

5 Bake for 20 to 25 minutes (mini loaves), 30 to 35 minutes (quarter loaves), or 1 hour (standard loaf), until a cake tester comes out clean. Set aside to cool, then drizzle with glaze and garnish with the remaining 1 tablespoon basil.

Store loaves, well wrapped, at room temperature for up to 2 days or in the freezer for up to 2 weeks.

Raspberry Loaf with Freeze-Dried Raspberry Glaze

Fresh raspberries at the height of summer pack a powerful flavor punch and we cram as many as we can in these farmers' market favorites. If you use frozen, be sure to find IQF (individually quick frozen) raspberries; otherwise, the berries might add too much moisture. Photographer, recipe tester, and quick bread guru Laura Scherb had the brilliant idea of using freeze-dried raspberries to make an intensely raspberry icing.

Ingredients

Yield: 8 mini loaves or 4 quarter loaves or 1 standard loaf

1 cup	**granulated sugar**	200g
3	**large eggs**	150g
1 cup	**crème fraîche**	240g
2¼ cups	**all-purpose flour**	270g
1 tablespoon	**baking powder**	12g
Pinch	**kosher salt**	
	Grated zest of 1 lemon	
¾ teaspoon	**vanilla paste, divided**	3.75g
1 cup	**fresh or IQF (individually quick frozen) raspberries**	125g
1 cup	**powdered sugar**	120g
2 tablespoons	**crushed freeze-dried raspberries**	10g
1 tablespoon	**lemon juice**	15g
1 tablespoon	**whole milk**	15g

1 Preheat the oven to 350°F. Prepare 8 mini loaf pans, 4 quarter loaf pans, or 1 standard loaf pan by greasing or lining with parchment paper.

2 In a large bowl, whisk together the granulated sugar and eggs until the mixture is pale and ribboned. Add the crème fraîche and mix well to incorporate. Whisk together the flour, baking powder, and salt and fold into the batter. Gently fold in the lemon zest and ½ teaspoon of the vanilla paste.

Next page

RASPBERRY LOAF WITH FREEZE-DRIED RASPBERRY GLAZE, *continued*

3 For each mini loaf, scoop 2 tablespoons batter into each pan, top with 2 tablespoons raspberries, then another 2 tablespoons batter. For each quarter loaf, scoop ¼ cup batter into each pan, top with ¼ cup raspberries, then another ¼ cup batter. For a standard loaf, scoop half of the batter into the pan, top with all the raspberries, then the remaining batter.

4 Bake for 20 to 25 minutes (mini loaves), 30 to 35 minutes (quarter loaves), or 1 hour (standard loaf), until a cake tester comes out clean. Set aside to cool.

5 To make the glaze, whisk together the powdered sugar, freeze-dried raspberries, lemon juice, milk, and remaining ¼ teaspoon vanilla paste until smooth. Drizzle over the cooled cakes.

Store loaves, well wrapped, at room temperature for up to 2 days or in the freezer for up to 2 weeks.

Rhubarb Loaf with Rhubarb Frosting

I like to peel the rhubarb to get rid of the tougher outer strings, though it is not strictly required. Use a sharp knife to cut the stalks into 1-inch pieces.

Ingredients

Yield: 8 mini loaves or 4 quarter loaves or 1 standard loaf

CAKE

1 cup	**granulated sugar**	200g
3	**large eggs**	150g
1 cup	**crème fraîche**	240g
2¼ cups plus 1 tablespoon	**all-purpose flour, divided**	275g
1 tablespoon	**baking powder**	12g
Pinch	**kosher salt**	
	Grated zest of 1 orange	
½ teaspoon	**vanilla paste**	2.5g
1 cup	**peeled and sliced fresh rhubarb**	125g

FROSTING

1 cup	**peeled and sliced fresh rhubarb**	125g
¼ cup	**orange juice**	60g
3 tablespoons	**granulated sugar**	38g
½ teaspoon	**vanilla paste**	2.5g
½ teaspoon	**ground ginger**	1g
3 ounces	**cream cheese, softened to room temperature**	85g
2 tablespoons	**unsalted butter, softened to room temperature**	28g
1¼ cups	**powdered sugar**	150g

Next page

RHUBARB LOAF WITH RHUBARB FROSTING, *continued*

1. Preheat the oven to 350°F. Prepare 8 mini loaf pans, 4 quarter loaf pans, or 1 standard loaf pan by greasing or lining with parchment paper.
2. To make the cake, in a large bowl, whisk together the granulated sugar and eggs until the mixture is pale and ribboned. Add the crème fraîche and mix well to incorporate. Combine 2¼ cups of the flour, the baking powder, and salt and fold into the batter until a few streaks of flour remain. Gently fold in the orange zest and vanilla paste just to incorporate.
3. Toss the rhubarb with the remaining 1 tablespoon flour to coat.
4. For each mini loaf, scoop 2 tablespoons batter into each pan, top with 2 tablespoons rhubarb, then another 2 tablespoons batter. For each quarter loaf, scoop ¼ cup batter into each pan, then ¼ cup rhubarb, then another ¼ cup batter. For a standard loaf, scoop half of the batter into the pan, then all the rhubarb, then the remaining batter.
5. Bake for 20 to 25 minutes (mini loaves), 30 to 35 minutes (quarter loaves), or 1 hour (standard loaf), until a cake tester comes out clean. Set aside to cool.
6. To make the frosting, combine the rhubarb, orange juice, granulated sugar, vanilla paste, and ground ginger in a medium saucepan and cook over medium heat, stirring occasionally, until the rhubarb has broken down into mush, about 5 minutes. Strain the mixture in a fine-mesh strainer set over a bowl, pressing the rhubarb pulp against the strainer to release the juices. Reserve the juices and discard the pulp. Cool.
7. In a medium bowl, using a hand mixer or stand mixer, cream together the cream cheese and butter until fluffy. Sift in the powdered sugar and whip until smooth. Add 3 tablespoons of the cooled rhubarb syrup and whip until smooth. Frost the cooled loaves.

Store loaves, well wrapped, at room temperature for up to 2 days or in the freezer for up to 2 weeks.

CHAPTER 5

Brioche

Don't let brioche intimidate you. Sure, it dates to the Middle Ages and has some history with Marie Antoinette, but the recipe, though long, is really quite simple. Follow the steps and you'll master it in no time. Brioche is a rich, slightly sweet yeast-risen bread whose light and airy texture belies the staggering amount butter and eggs we pack into the dough. The word *brioche* first appears in writing in 1404, but the original recipe is centuries older and much humbler. Generations of French bakers honed it, adding butter, eggs, and milk. While it most likely originated in Normandy, a dairy-rich region celebrated for its butter, it spread all across France. By the 1800s, most regions had their own signature preparation.

Simple Brioche Sandwich or Dinner Rolls (page 234)

Base Brioche Dough

Brioche is graded by the percentage of butter in the recipe compared to the amount of flour. Most brioche falls in the 50 to 70 percent range, though anything between 30 and 100 percent is possible. This recipe calls for 80 percent butter, putting it on the richer, denser side of the brioche scale. It works equally well for sandwich rolls as it does for pastries. The only real trick is ensuring the butter is at the perfect temperature before adding it to the dough. It should be softened but not greasy or partially melted.

Ingredients

Yield: 9 pieces

1¾ cups	**all-purpose flour, divided**	210g
1½ teaspoons	**instant yeast**	4.5g
4	**large eggs**	200g
¼ cup	**cool water (60 to 65°F)**	60g
2 tablespoons	**sugar**	25g
1 teaspoon	**kosher salt**	3g
1 cup (2 sticks) plus 3 tablespoons	**unsalted butter, softened to room temperature**	269g

1 Combine 1½ cups of the all-purpose flour, the yeast, eggs, and water in the bowl of a stand mixer. Mix with the paddle attachment on medium speed until smooth, about 1 minute. You may have to scrape down the sides of the bowl. Cover the bowl and let it stand for 45 minutes. The mixture will have a few bubbles but not rise much.

2 Add the remaining ¼ cup flour, the sugar, and salt to the mixture. Swap the paddle for the dough hook, then mix on medium speed for 8 to 10 minutes, until the dough cleans the sides of the bowl and becomes shiny and elastic. Add the very soft butter in small pieces and mix until the dough is shiny and very elastic and climbs the dough hook. This will take about 10 minutes. Test with the windowpane test (see sidebar).

3 Spray a medium bowl with cooking spray. Transfer the dough to the greased bowl. Cover and let stand at room temperature for 1 hour. Let proof in the refrigerator for at least 6 hours and up to 16 hours, then use in the following recipes.

All of the brioche recipes that follow can be made start to finish, or, once the brioche is shaped into balls, knots, or squares, you can loosely wrap them in plastic film and place them in the refrigerator overnight. In the morning, set the brioche in a warm spot to proof and proceed with the recipe. This is especially convenient when entertaining.

WINDOWPANE TEST

The windowpane test is an easy way bakers check for gluten development in their bread dough as it mixes. Dough passes the test when it can be pulled apart to form a membrane so thin you can see light through it. If the membrane tears, it goes back in the bowl to mix a bit longer. To perform the test, pinch off a small ball of dough, about the size of a ping-pong ball, and flatten it between your fingers. Grip opposite ends of the dough between your thumb and fingers. Slowly pull your hands apart so the center of the dough becomes thinner and thinner until you can see through it.

The airy, buttery texture of the Base Brioche Dough after proofing.

Simple Brioche Sandwich or Dinner Rolls

Don't worry if your first rolls end up more oblong than round. It takes some time to get a feel for shaping brioche. The good news is they're delicious no matter the shape!

Ingredients

Yield: 9 rolls

1 recipe	**Base Brioche Dough (page 232)**	
1	**large egg, lightly beaten**	50g
	kosher salt, freshly ground black pepper, poppy seeds, and/or sesame seeds, for topping (optional)	

1. Take the brioche dough out of the refrigerator and set aside until it is slightly cooler than room temp, 10 to 20 minutes. It will be easier to work with at this Goldilocks temperature.
2. Line 2 rimmed baking sheets with parchment paper. Divide the dough into 9 (3-ounce) portions. To roll each portion into a ball, slap it with the heel of your hand, flattening it slightly. Then, cup your hand over the dough, laying the sides of your thumb and pinkie on the work surface. Moving your arm from the shoulder, rotate your hand in increasingly smaller circles, drawing your fingers in to tighten the dough into a ball. Slap the dough again and repeat the process. (Slapping the dough releases air pockets that can cause large cavities when baked.) If the dough slides around too much to form a ball, mist the work surface with water. If the dough sticks to your hand or the work surface, dust it with a bit of flour.
3. Transfer the dough ball to the lined baking sheet and continue to form the remaining balls, placing 4 or 5 on each sheet. When all the rolls are shaped, spray the balls with water, wrap the baking sheets with plastic film and place in a warm spot to proof until roughly double in size, about 1 hour. The dough is ready when it slowly springs back when pressed.
4. Preheat the oven to 375°F.

5 Uncover the dough balls and gently brush with the egg wash. Top them with sesame seeds, poppy seeds, or whatever toppings you like. Bake until golden brown and an instant-read thermometer inserted in the center registers 190°F, 10 to 15 minutes. While the rolls can be eaten right away (and are delicious warm), let them cool fully before slicing.

While brioche is best eaten the day it is made, it can be stored well wrapped at room temperature for up to 2 days.

A shaped dough ball

All proofing times are guesstimates. Your senses of touch, sight, and smell are much more reliable indicators of when your dough is ready for the oven than time. Well-proofed dough feels bouncy but not squishy and springs back when lightly pressed. Your dough should look satiny but not greasy, and it should smell fresh and yeasty but not fermented or boozy.

Stuffed Brioche

Ingredients

Yield: 9 stuffed brioche rolls

1 recipe	**Base Brioche Dough (page 232)**
	Granulated sugar, for sprinkling
1 recipe	**Basic Pastry Cream (page 282), Chocolate Pastry Cream (page 284), Lemon Curd (page 277), Passion Fruit Curd (page 278), or Strawberry Jam (page 279)**

1. Follow instructions for Simple Brioche Sandwich or Dinner Rolls (page 234). Before placing the rolls in the oven, lightly brush with egg wash and sprinkle generously with granulated sugar.
2. Cool baked rolls to room temperature.
3. Fit a piping bag with Bismarck tip #232.
4. Fill the piping bag ⅔ full with basic pastry cream, chocolate pastry cream, lemon curd, passion fruit curd, or jam.
5. Insert the tip into the brioche. Lightly squeeze the pastry bag until the roll is filled. Remove any excess filling with an offset spatula.

Filled brioche may be left at room temperature for 2 hours. After that, store refrigerated for up to 2 days.

ORGANIC
FIRST QUALITY 1
Unsalted
PLANT #49-34
NET WT
4 OZ.
Sweet Cream
3 TBSP
4 TBSP
5 TBSP
6 TBSP
7 TBSP
1/4 CUP
1/3 CUP
THIS UNIT NOT LABELED FOR RETAIL SALE

Nutella/Peanut Butter Knots

A jar of Nutella is sold somewhere in the world every 2.5 seconds and a jar of peanut butter can be found in 75 percent of American homes, so it's no surprise these are our most popular pastries.

Ingredients

Yield: 9 pastries

1 recipe	**Base Brioche Dough (page 232)**	
1 cup	**Nutella or peanut butter**	280g
1 cup	**packed brown sugar**	213g
1	**large egg, beaten**	50g

Sanding sugar, for topping

Melted butter, for brushing

Chocolate chips or Peanut Streusel (page 55), for topping

1 Take the brioche dough out of the refrigerator and set aside until it is slightly cooler than room temp, 10 to 20 minutes. It will be easier to work with at this Goldilocks temperature.

2 Line a rimmed baking sheet with parchment paper. Divide the brioche dough into 9 (3-ounce) portions. Roll out each piece of dough into a rectangle that is roughly 7 × 5 inches. Place about 2 tablespoons Nutella or peanut butter in the center of the dough and use an offset spatula or butter knife to gently spread it out to the edges. Sprinkle 2 tablespoons brown sugar over the filling, spreading it evenly. Roll the dough toward you, starting with the long side of the rectangle to form a tube. Pinch the top of the tube to seal it.

3 Using a bench scraper or a large knife, start 1 inch from the top and cut down the middle of the roll to give you two halves. Separate the halves. Twirl each half over the other to make a twist and seal both ends. Tie the twist into an overhand knot so both tails are on the bottom. Pinch the tails together to seal and tuck under the knot. Transfer the dough knot to the lined baking sheet. Form the remaining knots, placing 4 or 5 on each sheet. When all the knots are shaped, spray them with water, wrap loosely with plastic wrap, and set aside in a warm spot to proof until roughly double in size, about 1 hour. The dough is ready when it slowly springs back when pressed.

4 Preheat the oven to 375°F.

5 Uncover the dough knots and gently brush with the egg wash and top with sanding sugar. Top Nutella knots with 1 tablespoon chocolate chips. Top peanut butter knots with 1 tablespoon peanut streusel. Bake for 10 to 15 minutes, until golden brown. Brush with melted butter and serve.

While brioche is best eaten the day it is made, it can be stored well wrapped at room temperature for up to 2 days.

Nutella Knots (page 238)

Raspberry Knots

These knots are delicious with any kind of jam. We are partial to raspberry and strawberry because we get such lovely berries from our farmers to make the jam. Store-bought works just fine too. Don't hesitate to experiment with more exotic flavors like guava, mango, or marmalades. The tartness of citrus marmalade is especially nice with the sweet pastry.

Yield: 9 pastries

1 recipe	**Base Brioche Dough (page 232)**	
1 cup	**raspberry jam**	320g
1 cup	**packed brown sugar**	213g
1	**large egg, beaten**	50g
	Sanding sugar, for topping	
	Melted butter, for brushing	

1 Take the brioche dough out of the refrigerator and set aside until it is slightly cooler than room temp, 10 to 20 minutes. It will be easier to work with at this Goldilocks temperature.

2 Line a rimmed baking sheet with parchment paper. Divide the brioche dough into 9 (3-ounce) portions. Roll out each piece of dough into a rectangle that is roughly 7 × 5 inches. Place about 2 tablespoons jam in the center of the dough and use an offset spatula or butter knife to gently spread it out to the edges. Sprinkle 2 tablespoons brown sugar over the filling, spreading it evenly. Roll the dough toward you, starting with the long side of the rectangle to form a tube. Pinch the top of the tube to seal it.

3 Using a bench scraper or a large knife, start 1 inch from the top and cut down the middle of the roll to give you two halves. Separate the halves. Twirl each half over the other to make a twist and seal both ends. Tie the twist into an overhand knot so both tails are on the bottom. Pinch the tails together to seal and tuck under the knot. Transfer the dough knot to the lined baking sheet. Form the remaining knots, placing 4 or 5 on each sheet.

4 When all the knots are shaped, spray them with water, wrap loosely with plastic film, and set aside in a warm spot to proof until roughly double in size, about 1 hour. The dough is ready when it slowly springs back when pressed.

5 Preheat the oven to 375°F.

6 Uncover the dough knots and gently brush with the egg wash and top with sanding sugar.

7 Bake for 20 to 25 minutes, until golden brown. Brush with melted butter and serve.

While brioche is best eaten the day it is made, it can be stored well wrapped at room temperature for up to 2 days.

VARIATION: Strawberry jam can be substituted for raspberry jam.

PB&J Knots

Who doesn't love PB&J? Are you a grown-up enjoying a sophisticated grown-up pastry with your coffee, as one does? Or are you indulging your inner child?

Ingredients

Yield: 9 pastries

1 recipe	**Base Brioche Dough (page 232)**	
½ cup	**peanut butter**	140g
½ cup	**raspberry or strawberry jam**	160g
1 cup	**packed brown sugar**	213g
1	**large egg, beaten**	50g
	Sanding sugar, for topping	
	Melted butter, for brushing	

1 Take the brioche dough out of the refrigerator and set aside until it is slightly cooler than room temp, 10 to 20 minutes. It will be easier to work with at this Goldilocks temperature.

2 Line a rimmed baking sheet with parchment paper. Divide the brioche dough into 9 (3-ounce) portions. Roll out each piece of dough into a rectangle that is roughly 7 × 5 inches. Place about 1 tablespoon peanut butter in the center of the dough and use an offset spatula or butter knife to gently spread it out to the edges. Spread about 1 tablespoon jam on top of the peanut butter, spreading as evenly as you can. Sprinkle 2 tablespoons brown sugar over the filling, spreading it evenly. Roll the dough toward you, starting with the long side.

3 Using a bench scraper or a large knife, start 1 inch from one end and cut all the way through the middle of the roll. Separate the halves. Twirl each half over each other to make a twist and seal both ends. Tie into an overhand knot so that both tails are on the bottom of the knot. Pinch them together to seal. Transfer the dough knot to the lined baking sheet and continue to form the remaining knots, placing 4 or 5 on each sheet. When all the knots are shaped, spray them with water, wrap loosely with plastic wrap, and set aside in a warm spot to proof for about 1 hour. The dough is ready when it slowly springs back when pressed.

4 Preheat the oven to 375°F.

5 Uncover the dough knots and gently brush with the egg wash and give a light sprinkling of sanding sugar.

6 Bake for 10 to 15 minutes, until golden brown. Immediately after baking, brush with melted butter and serve.

While brioche is best eaten the day it is made, it can be stored well wrapped at room temperature for up to 2 days.

Browned Butter Brioche Cinnamon Rolls

I find most cinnamon rolls overly sweet and, frankly, a little boring after that first sugary bite. Here the browned butter adds depth and complexity that balances the sweetness. Spring for the good cinnamon. Sharp, aromatic Vietnamese (also called Saigon) cinnamon works best.

Ingredients

Yield: 9 rolls

ROLLS

1 recipe	**Base Brioche Dough (page 232)**	
½ cup	**Browned Butter (page 293), cooled to a paste consistency**	113g
1 cup	**packed dark brown sugar**	213g
1 tablespoon	**ground cinnamon, preferably Vietnamese, plus more for dusting**	8g
Pinch	**kosher salt**	

CREAM CHEESE ICING

12 ounces	**cream cheese**	340g
½ cup	**Browned Butter (page 293)**	113g
2 pinches	**kosher salt**	
¼ teaspoon	**vanilla paste**	1.25g
2½ cups	**powdered sugar**	300g

1 Take the brioche dough out of the refrigerator and set aside until it is slightly cooler than room temp, 10 to 20 minutes. It will be easier to work with at this Goldilocks temperature.

2 Spray an 8 × 8-inch square baking pan or a 10-inch pie tin with cooking spray.

3 Roll out the brioche dough into a 12 × 18-inch rectangle about ⅓ inch thick. Using a pastry brush, brush the dough generously with the browned butter. Sprinkle the brown sugar all over the browned butter so that the dough below is barely showing. Sift or sprinkle the cinnamon on top of the brown sugar. Evenly distribute the salt over the dough.

Next page

BROWNED BUTTER BRIOCHE CINNAMON ROLLS, *continued*

4 Tightly roll up the sugared dough the long way, like a jelly roll, and seal the bottom as well as you can. Don't worry about the ends. Slice into 1½-inch rolls and place them cut sides down in the prepared pan. Spray the rolls with water, loosely wrap in plastic wrap, and set aside in a warm spot to proof, about 1 hour. When it's ready, the dough should barely spring back into shape when poked.

5 Preheat the oven to 350°F.

6 Uncover the rolls and bake for 20 to 25 minutes, until lightly browned. Cool.

7 To make the icing, combine all the ingredients in a food processor fitted with the blade attachment or a stand mixer fitted with the paddle attachment. Process or mix until the icing is smooth. Scoop the icing on top of the cooled cinnamon rolls and spread evenly. Dust with cinnamon. Serve.

While cinnamon rolls are best eaten the day they are made, they can be stored well wrapped at room temperature for up to 2 days.

Cream Cheese Brioche Danish

Danishes are typically made with a rich laminated dough that's closer to puff pastry than brioche. We love the airy fluffiness of brioche paired with the soft, lightly sweet cheese filling and didn't think anyone would mind if we stretched the definition a little—which is how we found ourselves being scolded by a gentleman one Saturday morning for both selling out of Danishes before he got one and "not making real Danishes anyway." These may not be real Danishes, but we think you will love them. Feel free to call them whatever you like.

Ingredients

Yield: 9 Danishes

DOUGH

1 recipe	**Base Brioche Dough (page 232)**	
1	**large egg, lightly beaten**	50g
	Sanding sugar, for sprinkling	
	Honey, for drizzling (optional)	

CREAM CHEESE DANISH FILLING

8 ounces	**cream cheese, softened to room temperature**	227g
1	**large egg yolk**	20g
½ teaspoon	**vanilla bean paste**	2.5g
¼ cup	**powdered sugar**	30g
2 pinches	**kosher salt**	

1 Take the brioche dough out of the refrigerator and set aside until it is slightly cooler than room temp, 10 to 20 minutes. It will be easier to work with at this Goldilocks temperature.

Next page

CREAM CHEESE BRIOCHE DANISH, *continued*

2 Line 2 rimmed baking sheets with parchment paper. Divide the brioche dough into 9 (3-ounce) portions. To roll each portion into a ball, slap it with the heel of your hand, flattening it slightly. Then, cup your hand over the dough, laying the sides of your thumb and pinkie on the work surface. Moving your arm from the shoulder, rotate your hand in increasingly smaller circles, drawing your fingers in to tighten the dough into a ball. Slap the dough again and repeat the process. (Slapping the dough releases air pockets that can cause large cavities when baked.) If the dough slides around too much to form a ball, mist the surface with water. If the dough sticks to your hand or the work surface, dust it with a bit of flour.

3 Transfer the dough ball to the lined baking sheet and continue to form the remaining Danishes, placing 4 or 5 on each sheet. When all the Danishes are shaped, wrap the baking sheets with plastic wrap and set aside to proof in a warm spot until doubled in size, about 1 hour.

4 Preheat the oven to 350°F.

5 To make the cream cheese Danish filling, in a handheld or stand mixer, cream the cream cheese, egg yolk, and vanilla together on medium speed. Add the powdered sugar and salt and continue mixing until smooth, scraping down the sides of the bowl to ensure everything is incorporated.

6 Once the dough is proofed, make an indentation in the middle of each dough ball using two or three fingers on each hand. Work the indentation into a circle, leaving a ¼- to ½-inch border all the way around. (Alternatively, press a ½-cup measure into the center of each dough ball.) Gently brush the pastries with the egg wash. Fill each indentation with 3 tablespoons cream cheese filling. Sprinkle the edges with sanding sugar.

7 Bake for 12 to 15 minutes, until golden brown and fragrant. Let cool to room temperature and drizzle with honey, if using.

Danishes are best eaten the day they are made, but you can store them tightly wrapped in the refrigerator overnight. To refresh, place a Danish on a plate next to a small bowl of water. Heat for 30 to 45 seconds in the microwave.

Apple Butter Danish

Credit Hoosier Mama pastry chef Marroz Franklin with thinking to combine homey, Midwestern apple butter with fancy French viennoiserie. The result is sophisticated comfort food. This is my favorite Danish!

Ingredients

Yield: 9 Danishes

1 recipe	**Base Brioche Dough (page 232)**	
1	**large egg, lightly beaten**	50g
2 cups	**Apple Butter (page 274)**	458g
	Sanding sugar, for sprinkling	

1. Take the brioche dough out of the refrigerator and set aside until it is slightly cooler than room temp, 10 to 20 minutes. It will be easier to work with at this Goldilocks temperature.
2. Line 2 rimmed baking sheets with parchment paper. Divide the brioche dough into 9 (3-ounce) portions. To roll each portion into a ball, slap it with the heel of your hand, flattening it slightly. Then, cup your hand over the dough, laying the sides of your thumb and pinkie on the work surface. Moving your arm from the shoulder, rotate your hand in increasingly smaller circles, drawing your fingers in to tighten the dough into a ball. Slap the dough again and repeat the process. (Slapping the dough releases air pockets that can cause large cavities when baked.) If the dough slides around too much to form a ball, mist the surface with water. If the dough sticks to your hand or the work surface, dust it with a bit of flour.
3. Transfer the dough ball to the lined baking sheet and continue to form the remaining Danishes, placing 4 or 5 on each sheet. When all the Danishes are shaped, wrap the baking sheets with plastic wrap and set aside to proof in a warm spot until doubled in size, about 1 hour.
4. Preheat the oven to 350°F.

5 Once the dough is proofed, make an indentation in the middle of each dough ball using two or three fingers on each hand. Work the indentation into a circle, leaving a ¼- to ½-inch border all the way around. (Alternatively, press a ½-cup measure into the center of each dough ball.)

6 Gently brush the pastries with the egg wash. Fill each indentation with 3½ tablespoons of the apple butter. Sprinkle the edges with sanding sugar.

7 Bake for 12 to 15 minutes, until golden brown and fragrant.

Danishes are best eaten the day they are made, but you can store them tightly wrapped in the refrigerator overnight. To refresh, place a Danish on a plate next to a small bowl of water. Heat for 30 to 45 seconds in the microwave.

Apple Butter (page 274)

Fruit Danish

Make these square, as described here, or round, following the instructions for Cream Cheese Brioche Danishes (page 249). Either way, they're delicious!

Ingredients

Yield: 9 Danishes

DANISH

1 recipe	**Base Brioche Dough (page 232)**
1 cup	**Blueberry Cobbler Filling (page 285) or Cherry Cobbler Filling (page 286)**

HONEY WASH

1 cup	**honey**	340g
⅓ cup	**warm water**	120g
	Granulated sugar, for topping	

1. Take the brioche dough out of the refrigerator and set aside until it is slightly cooler than room temp, 10 to 20 minutes.
2. Line 2 rimmed baking sheets with parchment paper. Divide the brioche dough into 9 (3-ounce) portions. Roll each portion into a 5 × 5-inch square, trimming the edges with a bench scraper or knife as necessary to get sharp corners and edges.
3. In a small bowl, stir together the honey and warm water until combined. Use a pastry brush to brush the brioche squares with honey wash. Reserve the remaining honey wash and store in the refrigerator until Danishes are ready to bake.
4. Add 2 tablespoons of the cobbler filling to the center of each square, and use an offset spatula or butter knife to spread the filling evenly over the dough, about ½ inch from the edges.
5. To shape each square, bring the opposite corners to the center, pressing lightly and using a damp finger if needed to stick the corners together in the middle of the pastry. Transfer to the lined baking sheet and continue to form the remaining Danishes, placing 4 or 5 on each sheet. When all the Danishes are shaped, spray with water, wrap with plastic film, and set aside in a warm spot to proof, about 1 hour. Dough is ready when it springs back slowly when pressed.

6 Preheat the oven to 350°F.

7 Uncover the dough balls, gently brush them all over with more honey wash, and sprinkle with granulated sugar.

8 Bake for 10 to 15 minutes, until golden brown and fragrant. Let cool before serving.

Danishes are best eaten the day they are made, but you can store them tightly wrapped in the refrigerator overnight. To refresh, place a Danish on a plate next to a small bowl of water. Heat for 30 to 45 seconds in the microwave.

DELUXE DANISHES

Danishes are incredibly versatile. You can have one topping, You can have two toppings. You can have two toppings plus a crumble and an icing drizzle. As a general guideline, the indentation holds 3 tablespoons of anything yummy. Try the Danish "formulas" below or build your own!

Flavor	Fillings	Toppings
Apple Butter & Walnut	• 3 tablespoons Apple Butter (page 274)	• Walnut Crumble (page 294)
Blueberry & Lemon	• 3 tablespoons Blueberry Cobbler Filling (page 285)	• Lemon Glaze (page 291)
Cherry & Walnut	• 3 tablespoons Cherry Cobbler Filling (page 286)	• Walnut Crumble (page 294)
Raspberry	• 3 tablespoons raspberry jam	• Simple Glaze (page 291)
Chocolate & Raspberry	• 1½ tablespoons Chocolate Pastry Cream (page 284) • 1½ tablespoons raspberry jam	
Chocolate-Raspberry & Almond	• 1½ tablespoons Chocolate Pastry Cream (page 284) • 1½ tablespoons raspberry jam	• 1½ tablespoons fresh raspberries (add to baked, cooled pastries) • Almond Glaze (page 291)
Chocolate-Nutella with Cinnamon & Espresso	• 1½ tablespoons Chocolate Pastry Cream (page 284) • 1½ tablespoons Nutella	• Cinnamon Streusel (page 276) • Espresso Glaze (page 291)
Chocolate & Passion Fruit Curd	• 1½ tablespoons Chocolate Pastry Cream (page 284) • 1½ tablespoons Passion Fruit Curd (page 278)	
Cream Cheese & Cherry	• 1½ tablespoons Cream Cheese Danish Filling (page 249) • 1½ tablespoons Cherry Cobbler Filling (page 286)	• Slivered almonds

Flavor	Fillings	Toppings
Cream Cheese & Blueberry	• 1½ tablespoons Cream Cheese Danish Filling (page 249) • 1½ tablespoons Blueberry Cobbler Filling (page 285)	
Cream Cheese–Cranberry with Walnut & Orange	• 1½ tablespoons Cream Cheese Danish Filling (page 249) • 1½ tablespoons Cranberry Sauce (page 288)	• Walnut Crumble (page 294) • Orange Glaze (page 291)
Cranberry-Marmalade	• 2 tablespoons Cranberry Sauce (page 288) • 1 tablespoon marmalade	• Chiffonade of Candied Orange Peel (page 296) (add to baked, cooled pastries)
Marmalade Crumble	• 3 tablespoons marmalade	• Oat Crumble (page 295)
Lemon Curd	• 3 tablespoons Lemon Curd (page 277)	
Lemon Curd & Blueberry	• 1½ tablespoons Lemon Curd (page 277) • 1½ tablespoons Blueberry Cobbler Filling (page 285)	
Lemon Curd & Raspberries	• 3 tablespoons Lemon Curd (page 277)	• 1 tablespoon fresh raspberries (add to baked, cooled pastries) • Simple Glaze (page 291)
Nutella & Cherry	• 1½ tablespoons Nutella • 1½ tablespoons Cherry Cobbler Filling (page 286)	
Passion Fruit Curd	• 3 tablespoons Passion Fruit Curd (page 278)	
Passion Fruit Curd & Blackberries	• 3 tablespoons Passion Fruit Curd (page 278)	• 1½ tablespoons fresh blackberries (add to baked, cooled pastries) • Simple Glaze (page 291)
Strawberry & Vanilla	• 1½ tablespoons Basic Pastry Cream (page 282) • 1½ tablespoons Strawberry Jam (page 279)	• 1½ tablespoons fresh strawberries (add to baked, cooled pastries) • Sherry Vinegar Icing (page 290)

Ham & Cheese Rolls

These are perfect for a fancy brunch or a handheld breakfast on the run. Shape them the night before and let them rest in the refrigerator overnight. Tasters were split on the addition of mustard. Mustard fans thought it brought out the cheddar flavor and added a nice tangy note. Non-fans said don't mess with the comfort-food perfection of classic ham and cheese. If in doubt, you can always offer it on the side after the rolls bake.

Ingredients

Yield: 12 rolls

1 recipe	**Base Brioche Dough (page 232)**	
¼ cup	**grainy Dijon mustard (optional)**	60g
2½ cups	**grated sharp cheddar cheese**	283g
6 ounces	**ham, sliced ⅛ inch thick**	170g
1	**large egg, beaten**	50g

1. Take the brioche dough out of the refrigerator and set aside until it is slightly cooler than room temp, 10 to 20 minutes. It will be easier to work with at this Goldilocks temperature.
2. Spray a 12-cavity jumbo muffin tin with cooking spray.
3. Liberally flour your work surface and roll the dough into a 15 × 24-inch rectangle with a long side near you. If using, spread the mustard as evenly as possible across the dough. Top with the cheddar cheese, leaving a ½-inch border on all four sides.
4. Starting ½ inch from the bottom of the dough, lay the ham out in two rows. Try not to overlap the ham slices. Fold the bottom ½-inch border up, then roll the dough into a log. Pinch the dough together along the seam and turn the log seam-side down.

Next page

HAM & CHEESE ROLLS, *continued*

5 If the log shrunk when you rolled it or is an uneven thickness, gently reshape it, squeezing and stretching it with your hands. It's OK if it ends up more square than round at this point. After proofing, it will fill the round muffin cups. Slice the log into 12 (2-inch) rounds. Place the rounds in the prepared muffin tin. Mist the rolls with water and cover loosely with plastic wrap.

6 Place the pan in a warm spot to proof for about 1 hour. The individual layers of brioche should double in width and feel spongy when poked.

7 Preheat the oven to 400°F.

8 Brush the tops of the rolls with the egg wash. Bake until dark golden brown, about 20 minutes. Serve rolls warm or cooled to room temperature.

Store the rolls, well wrapped, in the refrigerator for up to 2 days. To reheat, place a roll on a plate next to a small bowl of water and heat in the microwave for 45 seconds to 1 minute.

Spinach & Goat Cheese Rolls

Spinach and goat cheese is a classic combination. We added sweet caramelized onions to complement the tangy cheese. If, like some folks, you really can't stand goat cheese, substitute feta, fresh mozzarella, queso fresco, or European-style farmer cheese.

Ingredients

Yield: about 12 rolls

1 recipe	**Base Brioche Dough (page 232)**	
½ cup plus 3 tablespoons	**crème fraîche**	165g
¾ cup	**crumbled goat cheese**	85g
¾ cup	**shredded Gruyère cheese**	85g
½ cup	**Caramelized Onions (page 299)**	100g
1½ teaspoons	**granulated garlic**	6g
1¼ teaspoons	**kosher salt**	3.75g
¾ teaspoon	**freshly ground black pepper**	1.5g
5 ounces	**sautéed spinach**	142g
1	**large egg, beaten**	50g

1. Take the brioche dough out of the refrigerator and set aside until it is slightly cooler than room temp, 10 to 20 minutes. It will be easier to work with at this Goldilocks temperature.
2. Spray a 12-cavity jumbo muffin tin with cooking spray.
3. Combine the crème fraîche, goat cheese, Gruyère, caramelized onions, garlic powder, salt, and pepper in the bowl of a stand mixer fitted with the paddle attachment and mix on medium speed until well combined. Add the spinach and mix until incorporated.

Next page

SPINACH & GOAT CHEESE ROLLS, *continued*

4 Liberally flour your work surface and roll the dough into a 15 × 24-inch rectangle with a long side near you. Spread the cheese mixture as evenly as possible over the dough, leaving a ½-inch border on all four sides. Fold the bottom ½-inch border up, then roll the dough into a log. Pinch the dough together along the seam and turn the log seam-side down.

5 If the log shrunk when you rolled it or is an uneven thickness, gently reshape it, squeezing and stretching it with your hands. It's OK if it ends up more square than round at this point. After proofing, it will fill the round muffin cups. Slice the log into 12 (2-inch) rounds.

6 Place the rounds in the prepared muffin tin. Mist the rolls with water and cover loosely with plastic wrap. Place the pan in a warm spot to proof for about 1 hour. The individual layers of brioche should double in width and feel spongy when poked.

7 Preheat the oven to 400°F.

8 Brush the tops of the rolls with the egg wash. Bake until dark golden brown, about 20 minutes. Serve rolls warm or cooled to room temperature.

Store the rolls, well wrapped, in the refrigerator for up to 2 days. To reheat, place a roll on a plate next to a small bowl of water and heat in the microwave for 45 seconds to 1 minute.

Cranberry-Balsamic Bulgarian Feta Rolls

These are equally delightful as a breakfast pastry or an afternoon snack. Bulgarian Feta is creamier, sweeter, and less salty than Greek Feta. We make these at Christmastime, when cranberries are plentiful, but feel free to substitute cooked cherries or blueberries.

Yield: 12 rolls

Amount	Ingredient	Weight
1 recipe	**Base Brioche Dough (page 232)**	
1 (12-ounce) can	**cranberry sauce**	340g
½ cup	**Bulgarian Feta**	57g
2 tablespoons	**balsamic vinegar**	30g
1	**large egg, beaten**	50g

1. Take the brioche dough out of the refrigerator and set aside until it is slightly cooler than room temp, 10 to 20 minutes. It will be easier to work with at this Goldilocks temperature.
2. Spray a 12-cavity jumbo muffin tin with cooking spray.
3. In a medium bowl, mix the cranberry sauce, Feta, and balsamic vinegar until well combined. (Alternatively, use a stand mixer fitted with the paddle attachment and mix on medium speed.)
4. Liberally flour your work surface and roll the dough into a 15 × 24-inch rectangle with a long side near you. Spread the cranberry mixture as evenly as possible over the dough, leaving a ½-inch border on all four sides. Fold the bottom ½-inch border up, then roll the dough into a log. Pinch the dough together along the seam and turn the log seam-side down. If the log shrunk when you rolled it or is an uneven thickness, gently reshape it, squeezing and stretching it with your hands. It's OK if it ends up more square than round at this point. After proofing, it will fill the round muffin cups. Slice the log into 12 (2-inch) rounds.

5 Place the rounds in the prepared muffin tin. Mist the rolls with water and cover loosely with plastic wrap. Place the pan in a warm spot to proof for about 1 hour. The individual layers of brioche should double in width and feel spongy when poked.

6 Preheat the oven to 400°F.

7 Brush the tops of the rolls with the egg wash. Bake until dark golden brown, about 20 minutes. Serve rolls warm or cooled to room temperature.

Store the rolls, well wrapped, in the refrigerator for up to 2 days. To reheat, place a roll on a plate next to a small bowl of water and heat in the microwave for 45 seconds to 1 minute.

Sticky Buns

This recipe is a bit of a cheat. It produces a rich, buttery brioche-like dough with much less time and effort than actual brioche. In fact, most of your time is spent waiting for the dough to proof. It is inspired by King Arthur Baking's "Ridiculously Easy No-Knead Sticky Buns" and Jim Lahey of Sullivan Street Bakery's famous no-knead bread. The secret is a long, slow overnight rise after the dough is briefly mixed together. Resist the urge to overmix, knead, or fuss over this dough in any way. "Goo" is our in-house term for the maple-bourbon syrup that puts the sticky in sticky bun.

Ingredients

Yield: 9 jumbo sticky buns

DOUGH

2¼ teaspoons	**instant yeast**	7g
3¾ cups plus 2 tablespoons	**all-purpose flour**	464g
1¾ teaspoons	**kosher salt**	5.25g
¾ cup plus 2 tablespoons	**water, lukewarm (about 98°F)**	205g
2	**large eggs**	100g
¼ cup	**honey**	85g
¼ cup (½ stick)	**unsalted butter, melted**	57g

GOO

½ cup (1 stick)	**unsalted butter**	113g
¼ cup	**water**	60g
¼ cup	**heavy cream**	60g
¼ cup	**maple syrup**	85g
1 tablespoon	**bourbon**	15g
2¼ teaspoons	**vanilla paste**	11g
¾ teaspoon	**kosher salt**	2.25g
1 cup plus 2 tablespoons	**packed dark brown sugar**	240g

Next page

STICKY BUNS, *continued*

FILLING

1 cup	**packed dark brown sugar**	213g
1 cup	**granulated sugar**	200g
1½ teaspoons	**ground cinnamon**	4g
1 teaspoon	**kosher salt**	3g
3 cups	**pecans, toasted and chopped**	360g

TOPPING

1 heaping cup	**toasted pecans, roughly chopped**	~135g

1 To make the dough, coat a medium-sized mixing bowl with cooking spray. Set aside. Combine all the ingredients in the order listed in the bowl of a stand mixer fitted with the paddle attachment. Take care not to put the salt next to the yeast. Mix on medium speed until the dough comes together in a sticky mass and barely pulls away from the sides of the bowl, 2 to 3 minutes. Do not knead.

2 Transfer the dough to the prepared bowl, cover, and set aside at room temperature to proof for 2 hours. Transfer to the refrigerator and proof for an additional 6 to 24 hours.

3 To make the goo, combine all the ingredients in a large saucepan and heat over medium-low heat, stirring occasionally until the butter is melted and the mixture is well combined. Let cool to room temperature.

4 To make the filling, combine all the ingredients in a medium bowl, rubbing between your hands to combine thoroughly. Set aside.

5 To assemble the sticky buns, preheat the oven to 375°F. Remove the dough from the refrigerator. Coat 9 jumbo muffin tin cavities with cooking spray. Divide the toasted pecans between the muffin cups, adding about 2 tablespoons pecans to the bottom of each. Add 2 tablespoons goo to each muffin cup. Set aside, reserving the extra goo.

6 Turn the dough out onto a lightly floured surface and roll into a 12 × 18-inch rectangle. Spread the filling as evenly as possible over the dough.

7 Roll up the dough the long way, like a jelly roll, and shape to a uniform thickness. Using a serrated knife or a pizza cutter, cut the log into 9 (2-inch) pieces and place one in each muffin cup.

8 Cover with plastic wrap and place atop the oven to proof for about 20 minutes, or until the buns reach the plastic wrap.

9 Uncover the dough and brush the tops of the buns with about two-thirds of the remaining goo. Place the muffin tin on a parchment-lined baking sheet. Bake for 10 minutes, then take them out of the oven and brush with the remaining goo. Continue baking for 10 to 12 more minutes, until deeply browned and fragrant. Carefully turn them out of the muffin tin and scoop any extra nuts back onto the buns. Serve.

Store well wrapped at room temperature for up to 2 days. To refresh, place a sticky bun on a plate next to a small bowl of water. Heat for 30 to 45 seconds in the microwave.

Orange Sticky Buns

Ingredients

Yield: 9 jumbo sticky buns

1 recipe	**Sticky Bun Dough (see page 267)**	
1 recipe	**Sticky Bun Goo (see page 267)**	
2 ½ cups	**orange marmalade, divided**	640g
1 cup	**packed dark brown sugar**	213g

1 Preheat the oven to 375°F. Remove the dough from the refrigerator. Coat 9 jumbo muffin tin cavities with cooking spray. Add 2 tablespoons of the goo to the bottom of each muffin cup. Set aside.

2 Turn the dough out onto a lightly floured surface and roll into a 12 × 18-inch rectangle. Spread 2 cups of the marmalade as evenly as possible over the dough and top with the brown sugar.

3 Roll up the dough the long way, like a jelly roll, and shape to a uniform thickness. Using a serrated knife or a pizza cutter, cut the log into 9 (2-inch) pieces and place one in each muffin cup.

4 Cover with plastic wrap and place atop the oven to proof for about 20 minutes, or until the buns reach the plastic wrap.

5 Uncover the dough and brush the tops of the buns with about two-thirds of the remaining marmalade. Place the muffin tin on a parchment-lined baking sheet. Bake for 10 minutes, then take them out of the oven and brush with the remaining marmalade. Continue baking for 10 to 12 more minutes, until dark golden brown and fragrant, then carefully turn them out of the muffin tin. Serve.

Store well wrapped at room temperature for up to 2 days. To refresh, place a sticky bun on a plate next to a small bowl of water. Heat for 30 to 45 seconds in the microwave.

Raisin Rolls

Ingredients

Yield: 9 jumbo raisin rolls

1 recipe	**Sticky Bun Dough (see page 267)**	
1 recipe	**Sticky Bun Goo (see page 267)**	
1 cup	**raisins**	150g
2 tablespoons	**cognac or rum**	30g
1 cup	**Basic Pastry Cream (page 282)**	285g

1 Preheat the oven to 375°F. Remove the dough from the refrigerator. Coat 9 jumbo muffin tin cavities with cooking spray. Add 2 tablespoons of the goo to the bottom of each muffin cup. Set aside.

2 Measure the raisins into a small saucepan. Add the cognac and just enough water to cover. Bring to a boil. Remove from the heat and let stand, covered, for 10 minutes. Strain off any remaining liquid and set aside.

3 Turn the dough out onto a lightly floured surface and roll into a 12 × 18-inch rectangle. Spread the pastry cream as evenly as possible over the dough. Scatter the raisins over the pastry cream.

4 Roll up the dough the long way, like a jelly roll, and shape to a uniform thickness. Using a serrated knife or a pizza cutter, cut the log into 9 (2-inch) pieces and place one in each muffin cup.

5 Cover with plastic wrap and place atop the oven to proof for about 20 minutes, or until the buns reach the plastic wrap.

6 Uncover the dough and brush the tops of the buns with about two-thirds of the remaining goo. Place the muffin tin on a parchment-lined baking sheet. Bake for 10 minutes, then take them out of the oven and brush with the remaining goo. Continue baking for 10 to 12 more minutes, until dark golden brown and fragrant, then carefully turn them out of the muffin tin. Serve.

Store well wrapped at room temperature for up to 2 days. To refresh, place a raisin roll on a plate next to a small bowl of water. Heat for 30 to 45 seconds in the microwave.

CHAPTER 6

Additional Recipes

Apple Butter

Apple butter and biscuits is among the greatest food combinations of all time, so we knew we needed a killer apple butter recipe to go with our killer biscuits. This one is assertive, full of vinegary tang and sharp spices like cloves and black pepper. It's a bit intense on its own but mellows when paired with a buttery biscuit. It's all about the spice, so make sure you have good-quality, fresh spices on hand and spring for Vietnamese (also called Saigon) cinnamon if you can find it. It's strong and sweet, like Red Hots candies. You can use any apples you have on hand, but I like Granny Smith for the tart flavor!

Ingredients

Yield: about 1 quart

2 pounds (4–5 large)	**apples**	908g
¾ cup	**water**	180g
6 tablespoons	**apple cider vinegar**	90g
1½ cups	**granulated sugar**	300g
½ cup	**packed dark brown sugar**	106g
¾ teaspoon	**lemon juice**	3.75g
1 tablespoon	**honey**	21g
¾ teaspoon	**ground cinnamon, preferably Vietnamese**	1.8g
½ teaspoon	**ground cloves**	1g
¼ teaspoon	**ground allspice**	0.5g
⅛ teaspoon	**kosher salt**	0.3g
⅛ teaspoon	**freshly ground black pepper**	0.3g
1 teaspoon	**vanilla paste**	5g

If you don't let it scorch, apple butter is pretty forgiving. Apple butter that is too runny may be returned to the stove to cook longer. Apple butter that overthickens can be thinned with a bit of apple cider, apple juice, or water.

1 Rinse the apples and pat them dry. Cut the apples into quarters. Do not peel or core them. Combine the quartered apples, water, and vinegar in a medium, heavy-bottomed saucepan. Cook over high heat, stirring occasionally, until the mixture comes to a boil. Turn the heat down to medium, cover, and cook until the apples break down and the skin separates from the flesh, about 20 minutes.

2 Press the apples through a food mill or fine-mesh sieve. Return the apple puree to the saucepan and stir in both sugars, the lemon juice, honey, cinnamon, cloves, allspice, salt, and pepper. Cook over medium-high heat, stirring occasionally, until the mixture comes to a boil, 8 to 10 minutes. Turn the heat down to a simmer and continue cooking, stirring frequently to keep it from scorching. Reduce the heat as needed and cook until thickened, 35 to 45 minutes. The last 10 minutes or so should be spent over very low heat. Spoon a small amount of the apple butter onto a chilled plate or bowl to test the consistency. If the liquid separates from the apple butter, it needs more time.

3 Cool the apple butter to room temperature. Add the vanilla paste and adjust the seasoning to taste.

Store apple butter refrigerated in an airtight container for up to 1 week or freeze it for up to 3 months.

Cinnamon Streusel

Ingredients

Yield: about 1 cup

½ cup	**all-purpose flour**	60g
¼ cup	**granulated sugar**	50g
1 tablespoon	**packed dark brown sugar**	13g
Pinch	**kosher salt**	
¾ teaspoon	**ground cinnamon**	1.8g
3 tablespoons	**unsalted butter, cut into ½-inch cubes and chilled**	42g

1 Combine all ingredients in the bowl of a stand mixer fitted with the paddle attachment and mix on medium speed until crumbly.

Store refrigerated in an airtight container for up to 1 week.

Lemon Curd

My Evanston shop pastry chef, Marroz Franklin, developed this lovely lemon curd. It is extra creamy, extra lemony, thanks to the addition of lemon zest while it cooks, and just the right amount of tart. Enjoy it on biscuits, scones, and Danishes.

Ingredients

Yield: about 2 cups

1 cup	**granulated sugar**	200g
	Grated zest of 2 lemons	
5	**large egg yolks**	100g
7 tablespoons	**fresh lemon juice**	105g
½ cup (1 stick)	**unsalted butter, cut into ½-inch cubes and chilled**	113g

1. Combine the sugar and lemon zest in a small saucepan. Using your fingers, rub the lemon zest and sugar together until fragrant. Whisk in the egg yolks. Continue whisking until the mixture thickens and lightens in color, about 2 minutes. Slowly stir in the lemon juice.
2. Heat the mixture over low heat, whisking constantly, until it thickens enough to coat the back of a spoon, 8 to 10 minutes. Whisk the cold butter into the curd a few cubes at a time until well combined.
3. Strain the lemon curd through a fine-mesh sieve. Press a sheet of plastic wrap directly onto the surface of the lemon curd. This prevents a skin from forming. Let cool to room temperature.

Lemon curd can be stored in an airtight container in the refrigerator for up to 2 weeks or in the freezer for up to 2 months. To thaw, place it in the refrigerator for 24 hours before serving and use it within 1 week.

Passion Fruit Curd

Ingredients

Yield: about 1 quart

1 sheet	**leaf gelatin (silver strength)**	2.5g
9 ounces	**passion fruit puree**	293g
½ cup (1 stick) plus 2 tablespoons	**unsalted butter**	140g
½ cup plus 2 tablespoons	**sugar**	125g
Pinch	**kosher salt**	
10	**large egg yolks**	200g

1. Place the leaf gelatin in a small bowl of ice water. Set aside to bloom for 10 minutes.
2. Combine the passion fruit puree, butter, sugar, and salt in a medium, heavy-bottomed saucepan.
3. Place a fine-mesh strainer over the bowl of a stand mixer. Set the bowl close to the stove so you can strain the curd as soon as it is done cooking.
4. Place the saucepan over medium-high heat and cook until the sugar dissolves, the butter melts, and the mixture comes to a boil, about 3 minutes.
5. Meanwhile, place the egg yolks in a medium heatproof bowl and whisk until well combined.
6. Slowly pour the hot passion fruit mixture over the yolks, whisking constantly. Return the mixture to the saucepan. Cook over medium heat, whisking constantly, until the mixture thickens, about 2 minutes. Do not allow the mixture to boil. The curd is done when whisk tracks are visible for several seconds before disappearing, and the mixture easily coats the back of a spoon. Remove the curd from the heat.
7. Remove the leaf gelatin from the ice water. Wring out the excess water, then whisk the gelatin into the curd until it dissolves. Pour the curd through the strainer into the mixer bowl. Place the bowl back on the stand mixer fitted with the whisk attachment. Whisk on low speed until the mixture begins to cool and thicken. Turn up the speed to high and whisk until the mixer bowl is cool to the touch.

The finished curd can be stored in an airtight container in the refrigerator for up to 1 week.

Strawberry Jam

This is my go-to all-purpose jam. It's great on biscuits, as a Danish topping, or as the filling in corn muffins (page 45). You don't taste the balsamic vinegar itself in the finished jam. It is a supporting act that intensifies the flavor and makes even meh berries taste great. If, like me, you like that balsamic tang, you can swap out 2 tablespoons of the lemon juice for an additional 2 tablespoons of vinegar. An acidic jam tastes great with buttery biscuits.

Ingredients

Yield: about 3 cups

3 pounds	**fresh or IQF (individually quick frozen) strawberries, hulled and cut into halves or quarters**	1,360g
1½ pounds	**sugar**	680g
Pinch	**kosher salt**	
1½ teaspoons	**freshly ground black pepper**	3g
½ cup	**lemon juice**	120g
2 tablespoons	**balsamic vinegar**	30g

1. Place a plate or small metal bowl in the freezer.
2. Combine the berries, sugar, salt, pepper, lemon juice, and balsamic vinegar in a heavy-bottomed 7- to 8-quart saucepan. Stir the mixture until the strawberries release their juices and form a paste with the sugar, vinegar, and lemon juice.
3. Bring to a boil over medium-high heat, stirring occasionally so the fruit does not scorch and the sugar dissolves in the fruit juices, about 10 minutes. Turn the heat down to a vigorous simmer. Small bubbles will cover most of the surface. Stir the jam every few minutes, mashing some of the berries against the side of the pot. Adjust the temperature as needed. After 15 to 20 minutes, the jam will thicken dramatically, and the bubbles will get larger. The color will intensify, and the jam will become translucent. Turn the heat down to low and continue cooking until the jam reaches 220°F on a candy or instant-read thermometer. For a smoother jam, stir the mixture with a whisk to break up more of the fruit.

Next page

STRAWBERRY JAM, *continued*

4 Remove the jam from the heat. Spoon a few tablespoons of jam onto the chilled plate and return to the freezer. After 2 to 3 minutes, make a line through the jam with your finger. If the jam wrinkles and does not fill in the line, it is done. If the jam is still runny, return it to the stove, cook for another 5 minutes, and test again.

5 Cool the finished jam over an ice bath and transfer it to a quart container with a lid.

Store jam refrigerated for up to 1 week or in the freezer for up to 3 months.

If you plan to make jam often, buy a couple of extra-long-handled metal "Lunch Lady" spoons. The jam will bubble and spit as it gets close to temperature, and jam burns are no joke! The spoons usually have a hole in the handle. Slip your instant-read thermometer through the hole in your spare (nonstirring) spoon and hold on to the spoon bowl to keep your hands away from the steam.

Basic Pastry Cream

Most new pastry cooks are intimidated by pastry cream. I was too, but if you follow all the steps, there is really nothing to it. The only tricky part for a newbie is determining when the cream is cooked just enough—but not too much. Properly cooked pastry cream is glossy, while undercooked cream looks dull and chalky. If you are unsure, keep a spoon handy and taste it. If the cornstarch has not cooked off, the cream will taste dull and feel powdery or pasty on your tongue. Cook it a little longer and taste it again.

Ingredients

Yield: about 3 cups

½ sheet	**leaf gelatin (silver strength)**	1.25g
3 cups	**whole milk, divided**	720g
1 tablespoon	**unflavored powdered gelatin**	7g
1 cup	**sugar**	200g
¼ cup	**cornstarch**	35g
3	**large egg yolks**	60g
1	**large egg**	50g
2 tablespoons	**unsalted butter**	28g
1 tablespoon	**vanilla paste**	15g
1 cup	**heavy cream**	232g

1 Place the leaf gelatin in a small bowl of ice water. Set aside to bloom for 10 minutes.

2 Pour ½ cup of the milk into a small bowl. Sprinkle the powdered gelatin over the milk and let stand for 10 minutes.

3 Combine the milk-gelatin mixture with the remaining 2½ cups milk in a medium, heavy-bottomed saucepan. Whisk over medium-high heat until the powdered gelatin dissolves, about 1 minute. Continue to heat, whisking occasionally, until the mixture is just below a boil and small bubbles are forming along the side of the saucepan, about 4 minutes.

4 Meanwhile, place the sugar and cornstarch in a small bowl and whisk to combine.

5 In a large heatproof bowl, combine the egg yolks and egg. Whisk in the sugar and cornstarch mixture. Gradually, in several additions, whisk in the hot milk mixture.

6 Pour everything back into the saucepan and whisk constantly over medium heat until the mixture starts to thicken and boil, 1½ to 2 minutes. Whisk at a boil for 2 more minutes. Remove from the heat.

7 Remove the leaf gelatin from the water. Wring out the excess water, then whisk the gelatin into the pastry cream until it dissolves. Whisk in the butter and vanilla paste.

8 Pour the pastry cream through a fine-mesh strainer into a heatproof bowl. Press a piece of plastic wrap directly onto the surface of the pastry cream and gently smooth with your fingers. This will prevent a skin from forming. Chill in the refrigerator until the pastry cream is firm, about 2 hours. You can speed up this process by placing the pastry cream over an ice-water bath.

9 Pour the heavy cream into the bowl of a stand mixer fitted with the whisk attachment. Whip on medium speed for 30 seconds. Mix on high until soft peaks form, 1½ to 2 minutes.

10 Remove the firm pastry cream from the refrigerator. Remove the plastic wrap and set it aside. Whisk the pastry cream until smooth, then gradually fold in the whipped cream until no streaks remain. Smooth the top of the pastry cream and re-cover with the plastic wrap. Chill in the refrigerator until the pastry cream is set, about 1 hour.

The pastry cream can be made 1 day ahead and stored in an airtight container in the refrigerator.

Chocolate Pastry Cream

Ingredients

Yield: about 3 cups

1 cup	**whole milk, divided**	242g
½ cup	**heavy cream**	116g
1½ tablespoons	**cornstarch**	13.5g
1	**large egg**	50g
¼ cup	**sugar**	50g
2½ ounces	**semisweet chocolate, roughly chopped**	71g
2½ ounces	**bittersweet chocolate, roughly chopped**	71g
2 tablespoons	**unsalted butter**	28g
1 teaspoon	**vanilla paste**	10g
2 pinches	**kosher salt**	

1. Combine ¾ cup of the milk and the heavy cream in a small, heavy-bottomed saucepan. Bring to a boil over medium-high heat, stirring occasionally so the milk does not scorch on the bottom of the pan.

2. Meanwhile, in a small bowl, whisk the remaining ¼ cup milk into the cornstarch to make a smooth slurry.

3. Crack the egg into a medium, deep heatproof bowl. Whisk in the sugar until well combined. Slowly pour the slurry into the egg mixture and whisk until smooth. Gradually whisk in the hot milk mixture, stirring until well combined.

4. Pour everything back into the saucepan and cook over medium heat, whisking constantly, until it starts to thicken and just begins to boil, 1½ to 2 minutes. Whisk at a boil for 2 more minutes.

5. Remove the saucepan from the heat and add both of the chocolates and the butter. Whisk until everything is melted and well incorporated. Whisk in the vanilla paste and salt.

6. Pour the pastry cream through a fine-mesh strainer into a heatproof bowl. Press a piece of plastic wrap directly onto the surface of the pastry cream. This will prevent a skin from forming. Chill in the refrigerator until it is firm, about 2 hours. You can speed this process by placing the bowl of pastry cream over an ice-water bath.

The chocolate pastry cream can be made up to 1 day in advance and stored in an airtight container in the refrigerator.

Blueberry Cobbler Filling

Cooking blueberries produces a lot of juice, which is a good thing for flavor but a bad thing for consistency. We use tapioca starch (also called tapioca flour or cassava flour) anytime we cook blueberries. It thickens like crazy, has no discernable flavor, and adds a nice shine. If your local grocer doesn't carry it, try an Asian market, health food store, or Whole Foods.

Ingredients

Yield: about 2½ cups

1½ cups	**sugar**	260g
6 tablespoons	**tapioca starch**	43g
Pinch	**kosher salt**	
6 cups	**IQF (individually quick frozen) blueberries**	900g
	Grated zest of 1 lemon	
2 teaspoons	**fresh lemon juice**	10g

1. Preheat the oven to 375°F. Coat a 2-quart baking dish with cooking spray.
2. In a small bowl, whisk together the sugar, tapioca starch, and salt.
3. Put the blueberries in the prepared baking dish. Zest the lemon over the blueberries. Add the lemon juice. Add the tapioca starch mixture and toss to combine.
4. Bake, stirring every 10 minutes, until the mixture thickens and becomes shiny and translucent, about 30 minutes.

Store the blueberry cobbler filling in an airtight container in the refrigerator for up to 1 week.

Cherry Cobbler Filling

This is a recipe rock star. We use it in pies, pastries, muffins, cobblers, and Danishes. We pair it with yogurt and granola and spoon it onto biscuits. It's fantastic over ice cream and pound cake—you get the idea. Keep some on hand and see what you come up with.

Ingredients

Yield: about 2½ cups

½ cup plus 2 tablespoons	**sugar**	100g
2 tablespoons	**cornstarch**	16g
¾ teaspoon	**tapioca starch**	2g
Pinch	**kosher salt**	
5 cups	**IQF (individually quick frozen) cherries**	800g
½ teaspoon	**vanilla or almond extract**	2.5g

1. Preheat the oven to 375°F. Coat a 2-quart baking dish with cooking spray.
2. In a small bowl, whisk together the sugar, cornstarch, tapioca starch, and salt.
3. Put the cherries in the prepared baking dish. Add the vanilla or almond extract. Add the cornstarch mixture and toss to combine.
4. Bake, stirring every 10 minutes, until the mixture thickens and becomes shiny and translucent, about 30 minutes.

Store the cherry cobbler filling in an airtight container in the refrigerator for up to 1 week.

Cranberry Sauce

Let me use this space to shill for cranberries. They are delicious—tart, slightly astringent, bright, and fresh. They bring high-energy drama to a season of beige apple and pear dishes. Yet, people fear them. To answer one common concern: No, they are not too tart unless you prepare them that way. Like lemons, cranberries require a lot of sweetening. Use this as an excuse to layer in sweet flavors in addition to sugar, like honey, maple syrup, apple cider, or orange juice.

Ingredients

Yield: about 2 cups

5 cups	**fresh or frozen cranberries**	575g
1½ cups	**sugar**	300g
Pinch	**kosher salt**	
¾ teaspoon	**ground cinnamon**	1.8g
½ teaspoon	**ground nutmeg**	1g
⅛ teaspoon	**ground cloves**	0.25g
⅛ teaspoon	**freshly ground black pepper**	0.3g
¾ cup	**orange juice**	180g

1 Combine all the ingredients in a medium, heavy-bottomed saucepan. Heat over medium heat, stirring occasionally, until the cranberries pop and the sauce thickens, about 10 minutes.

Store the cranberry sauce in an airtight container in the refrigerator for up to 1 week.

Popped Pumpkin Seeds

Some seeds will audibly pop and jump off the pan. Others will just puff up in size. Either way, they are delicious. We use these to top our pumpkin cream cheese muffins and pumpkin sticky buns. Sometimes, we make extra just for snacking.

Ingredients

Yield: about ¼ cup

2 tablespoons	**canola oil**	28g
¼ cup	**raw, unsalted pumpkin seeds**	32g
½ teaspoon	**kosher salt**	1.5g

1. Line a plate or rimmed baking sheet with paper towels.
2. Heat the oil in an 8- to 10-inch skillet or saucepan over high heat until shimmering. Place one or two pumpkin seeds in the oil. When the seeds pop or puff up to double in size, add the rest of the pumpkin seeds. Shake the pan until all of the seeds have either popped or doubled in size, about 30 seconds. Turn the seeds out onto the paper towels and sprinkle with the salt.

Store in an airtight container at room temperature for up to 1 week.

Sherry Vinegar Icing

This recipe makes more than you need, but reducing less than a cup of vinegar without burning down your kitchen is hard!

Ingredients

Yield: about 1½ cups

1 cup	**sherry vinegar**	240g
2½ cups	**powdered sugar**	300g
2 tablespoons	**whole milk**	30g

1. Bring the sherry vinegar to a boil in a small, heavy saucepan over high heat. Turn the heat down to medium-low and simmer to reduce liquid to ¼ cup, 10 to 12 minutes. Set aside to cool slightly.
2. Put the powdered sugar in a medium bowl. Slowly whisk in the reduced vinegar and milk until smooth. The icing will be quite thick.
3. Place the bowl over a bowl of hot water and whisk until it is loose enough to fall from the tines of a fork or whisk. Use right away to drizzle over pastry.

Store the icing in an airtight container in the refrigerator for up to 1 week or in the freezer for up to 3 months. Thaw in the refrigerator overnight. When ready to use, whisk over a bowl of hot water as directed above.

Simple Glaze

This is our go-to quick and easy glaze recipe. We mix it up thick, then gently warm it to "drizzle" consistency. It sets up firm in a few minutes at room temperature.

Ingredients

Yield: about 2 cups

2 cups	**powdered sugar**	240g
¼ cup	**whole milk**	60g

1 In a small bowl, whisk together the powdered sugar and milk until smooth. If the glaze is too thick, add milk 1 teaspoon at a time until you reach the desired consistency. Remember to test the consistency warmed before adding extra liquid. Drizzle over pastry.

You can make the glaze up to 1 week in advance and store it in an airtight container in the fridge. When you are ready to use the glaze, warm it gently over a hot water bath, stirring frequently, or in a microwave, heating it for a few seconds at a time until it is spreadable.

ORANGE VARIATION: Replace 2 tablespoons of the whole milk with freshly squeezed orange juice.

LEMON VARIATION: Replace 2 tablespoons of the whole milk with freshly squeezed lemon juice.

PEACH VARIATION: Replace 2 tablespoons of the whole milk with peach juice.

ALMOND VARIATION: Add ¼ teaspoon almond extract.

ESPRESSO VARIATION: Replace 2 tablespoons of the whole milk with 1 shot of espresso or 2 tablespoons of strong coffee or cold brew.

Cream Cheese Filling

This is the cream cheese filling we use for our Pumpkin Cream Cheese Muffins (page 60) and Rainbow Carrot Cake Muffins (page 63). Don't confuse it with the Cream Cheese Brioche Danish (page 249) filling.

Ingredients

Yield: about 3 cups

1 pound	**cream cheese, softened to room temperature**	454g
1¾ cups	**sugar**	350g
	Grated zest of 2 oranges	
¼ cup	**sour cream**	60g
1	**large egg**	50g
1 teaspoon	**vanilla paste**	5g

1 In the bowl of a stand mixer fitted with the paddle attachment, cream the cream cheese, sugar, and orange zest on medium speed until fluffy and light. Add the sour cream, egg, and vanilla paste and continue mixing, scraping down the bowl after each addition, until smooth.

Store refrigerated in an airtight container for up to 1 week.

Browned Butter

Browned butter is kitchen magic, adding a nutty, rich complexity to everything from cinnamon rolls to sautéed veggies. Once you master the process, you'll want to add it to everything!

Ingredients

Yield: about 1½ cups

1 pound (2 cups/4 sticks)	**unsalted butter, cubed**	454g

1 Place a heatproof bowl of ice and a dry, empty heatproof bowl next to the stove. This will be your ice bath, so you can cool the browned butter quickly. Don't set the dry bowl in the bowl of ice yet. Condensation could cause water to accumulate in the bottom, making the hot browned butter pop and spatter when poured into the bowl.

2 Place the cubed butter in a light-colored, heavy-bottomed saucepan or skillet. A wider pan will allow the butter to cook more evenly. Heat the butter over low heat, stirring occasionally with a wooden spoon or silicone spatula until completely melted. Turn up the heat to medium and continue stirring occasionally and scraping down the sides and bottom of the pan as the butter comes to a boil. After about 5 minutes, the butter will foam and must be watched very closely. Flecks of caramelized milk fat will appear in the foam. You might have to push the foam away from the center of the pan or briefly remove the pan from the heat to see it. Keep scraping the bits of milk fat from the bottom of the pan.

3 When the flecks are the color of toffee, your butter is done. Remove the pan from the heat and pour the butter into the dry bowl. Be sure to scrape up the caramelized bits from the bottom of the pan. Be careful; the butter is over 200°F at this point! Place the bowl of butter in the bowl of ice and stir for a minute or two to stop the cooking. When the butter is cool enough to work with but still liquid, you can add it to your recipe.

Cool the browned butter completely, then store in an airtight container in the refrigerator for up to 1 week or in the freezer for up to 2 months. Gently warm refrigerated or frozen browned butter in a saucepan over low heat to return it to a liquid state before use.

Nut Crumble

Most often, we make this recipe with walnuts or pecans, but feel free to get creative. Hazelnuts, macadamia nuts, almonds, and pine nuts all make yummy variations.

Ingredients

Yield: about 2 cups

½ cup plus 2 tablespoons	**all-purpose flour**	81g
⅓ cup	**granulated sugar**	67g
1 tablespoon	**packed dark brown sugar**	13g
Pinch	**kosher salt**	
⅓ cup	**pecans or walnuts, roughly chopped**	40g
¼ cup (½ stick)	**unsalted butter, cut into ½-inch cubes and chilled**	57g

1 Combine the flour, granulated sugar, brown sugar, salt, and nuts in the bowl of a stand mixer fitted with the paddle attachment or in a small mixing bowl. Mix on low speed to combine. Add the butter and mix on high speed until the mixture just begins to get clumpy, about 10 minutes. (Alternatively, combine the flour, sugars, salt, and nuts in a medium bowl. Rub the butter cubes into the flour mixture with your hands or mash with a fork until the mixture resembles a coarse meal.)

Store the crumble in an airtight container in the refrigerator for up to 1 week or in the freezer for up to 2 weeks.

Oat Crumble

This crumble is especially good with apples and rhubarb. I like it best made with old-fashioned rolled oats, but you can substitute quick-cooking oats in a pinch. Do not use instant or steel-cut oats.

Ingredients

Yield: about 2 cups

1 cup	**old-fashioned oats**	90g
½ cup	**packed dark brown sugar**	106g
¼ cup	**all-purpose flour**	30g
¾ teaspoon	**kosher salt**	2.25g
¼ cup (½ stick)	**unsalted butter, cut into ½-inch cubes and chilled**	57g

1 Combine the oats, brown sugar, flour, and salt in the bowl of a stand mixer fitted with the paddle attachment. Mix on low speed to combine. Add the butter and mix on high speed until the mixture just begins to get clumpy, about 10 minutes. (Alternatively, combine the oats, brown sugar, flour, and salt in a medium bowl. Rub the butter cubes into the flour mixture with your hands or mash with a fork until the mixture resembles a coarse meal.)

Store the crumble in an airtight container in the refrigerator for up to 1 week or in the freezer for up to 2 weeks.

Candied Orange Peel

Although candying orange peel takes a bit of time, the result is well worth it. This recipe makes more than you need to mix into a scone or top a Danish, but smaller batches are harder to control. You'll find lots of uses for the extra. In fact, I developed the White Chocolate & Orange Rye Scones (page 115) to use up candied peel left over from mincemeat pie production. Add it to muffins or cookies. Slice into thin strips to garnish cocktails, or dip it in chocolate to make your own candy.

Ingredients

Yield: about 1½ cups

3	**large oranges, rinsed and quartered**	447g
4 cups	**sugar**	800g

1 Remove the orange peels by running your thumb between the white pith and orange pulp. Set the pulp aside for another use or discard. Place the orange peels in a 4-quart saucepan. Cover with 8 cups cold water and add a few ice cubes. Bring to a boil over medium heat.

2 Remove the pot from the stove and carefully drain the boiling water. Re-cover with 8 cups fresh cold water and a few ice cubes, bring to a boil, and drain. Repeat 3 more times so that the peel has been boiled 5 times.

3 After the fifth boil, drain the hot water and add the sugar and 4 cups fresh cold water. Stir just until the sugar is suspended in the water.

4 Return the pan to the stove and bring to a boil over high heat. Reduce the heat and simmer until the sugar syrup thickens and reduces by roughly half, about 35 minutes. The syrup will be golden brown and smell like caramel and the orange peel will be translucent. Cool to room temperature.

5 Remove the orange peels from the syrup and chop for immediate use. Use the leftover syrup to flavor lemonade, tea, and coffee or make an Italian soda. It's also great drizzled over pancakes, waffles, and ice cream or mixed into a cocktail.

If you are not using them right away, store the candied peels in the syrup in an airtight container in the refrigerator for up to 3 weeks.

Sautéed Collard Greens

If you have never tried collard greens, you are in for a treat. They cook up meaty and satisfying. Feel free to substitute turnip, mustard, or dandelion greens—from a trusted culinary source, of course.

Ingredients

Yield: about 1½ cups

2 tablespoons plus 1½ teaspoons	**kosher salt, divided**	19.5g
1 pound	**collard greens**	454g
2 cloves	**garlic**	10g
3 tablespoons	**bacon fat**	42g
½ teaspoon	**freshly ground black pepper**	1g

1. Fill a large pot with 3 quarts water plus 2 tablespoons of the salt. Bring to a boil over high heat. Prepare a large bowl of ice water.
2. Wash the collard greens in cool running water. Remove the woody stems by placing each leaf on a cutting board and running a sharp paring knife down both sides of the center stem. Discard the stems.
3. Add the greens to the boiling water and blanch for 3 minutes. Start counting the blanching time when the water returns to a boil. Dunk the greens back under the water as needed with tongs or a slotted spoon. After 3 minutes, plunge the greens into the ice water. Drain the greens and pat dry.
4. Mince the garlic with a chef's knife. Add ½ teaspoon of the salt and work into a rough paste with the side of the knife.
5. Heat the bacon fat in a large sauté pan or skillet over medium-high heat. Add the garlic paste and cook until fragrant, about 20 seconds. Add the collard greens and toss to coat the leaves with fat. Turn the heat down to medium. Add the remaining 1 teaspoon salt and the pepper and sauté until the greens are bright green and glossy but still have some bite, 10 to 12 minutes. Add 1 or 2 tablespoons water if the greens start to stick to the pan. Use right away, or spread the greens out on a rimmed baking sheet to cool.

Store the sautéed greens in an airtight container in the refrigerator for up to 5 days or in the freezer for up to 1 month.

Roasted Garlic

Roasting garlic mellows and deepens the flavor. Once you try it, you'll find yourself swapping in roasted garlic for fresh garlic in all kinds of recipes.

Ingredients

Yield: about 1 cup

1 head	**garlic**	~40g
1 tablespoon	**olive oil**	14g

1. Preheat the oven to 400°F. Cut the garlic head in half crosswise and place in a small baking dish. Drizzle with the olive oil and wrap the entire dish in aluminum foil. Roast for 50 to 60 minutes, until the garlic is completely soft. Unwrap carefully and set aside to cool.
2. Squeeze the garlic cloves from their papery skins. Discard the skins and smash the garlic cloves with a fork or puree in a food processor. Use right away or cool and then store for later use.

If you're not using the roasted garlic right away, store it in an airtight container in the refrigerator for up to 1 week. Freezing small blocks in an ice cube tray is also a good way to save excess. Once frozen, transfer to a resealable freezer bag or airtight container and store in the freezer for up to 3 months.

Caramelized Onions

Caramelizing onions is time-consuming but simple. Luckily, you don't have to hover over the stove the whole time. Make these a day ahead, or make a large batch and freeze what you don't use right away.

Ingredients

Yield: 2½–3 cups

½ cup (1 stick)	**unsalted butter**	113g
¼ cup	**olive oil**	55g
8	**medium yellow onions, peeled and cut into ¼-inch-thick slices**	1.6 kg

1 Heat the butter and olive oil in a large, heavy skillet over medium-low heat. Once the butter is melted, stir in the sliced onions to coat them. Cover the pan and cook until the unions are translucent and soft, 15 to 20 minutes.

2 Remove the lid and turn the heat up to medium. Continue cooking for about 1 hour, stirring every 10 minutes or so to brown the onions evenly. If the onions begin to burn, add a splash of water to slow their cooking. Stir often, adding more olive oil if the onions begin to stick. The onions are ready when they're a deep brown color and taste rich and sweet. Sometimes this takes longer than an hour. Judge the onions' doneness by color rather than by the clock! Use right away or cool and then store for later use.

Store caramelized onions in an airtight container in the refrigerator for up to 1 week. Freezing the onions in 1-cup servings in resealable freezer bags is convenient, and they will keep for 6 to 8 weeks.

CAKE
THE GREAT FOOD ALMANAC
CHEESE PRIMER
BAKING ILLUSTRATED
CHARLESTON RECEIPTS
SETTLEMENT COOKBOOK
COUNTRY COOKBOOK
Slow Cooker

ACKNOWLEDGMENTS

Unlike the proverbial broth, this book benefitted from many, many cooks in the kitchen. Thanks to Laura Scherb (laura@pageandplate.com) for the beautiful photographs, recipe testing, and general nudging to get the project done. Thanks to the patient folks at Agate for working around our baking schedule and for the years the book was in the talking stages. Special thanks to Olivia Sweets and Abigale Murabito at the Chicago shop, and Marroz Franklin and Heather Hamilton at the Evanston location for handling the day-to-day so I could write, and for fielding random texts at odd hours about egg washes, biscuit sizes, and baking times. Finally, a sincere thank you to all Hoosier Mamas (and Papas) past and present for making mornings at the pie shop so special.

FRIGIDAIRE RECIPES
THE DAIRY COOK BOOK
CULINARY ARTS INSTITUTE
THE AFTERNOON TEA BOOK
MICHAEL SMITH
BEARD ON BREAD
JAMES BEARD
KNOPF
ON FOOD AND COOKING
HAROLD McGEE
THE FANNIE FARMER BAKING BOOK
Marion Cunningham

REFERENCES

Addison, Esme. "Biscuits: A History of English & Scottish Immigration to the South." *Due South*, March 9, 2023. https://duesouth.media/biscuits-a-delicious-culinary-history-of-english-scottish-immigration-to-the-south/.

Amick, Brian. "Biscuits Bring Major Appeal to Menus." *Bake*, September 27, 2022. https://www.bakemag.com/articles/16619-biscuits-bring-major-appeal-to-menus.

Andolina, Heather. "Melungeon Heritage." *Black by God/The West Virginian*, May 1, 2023. https://blackbygod.org/articles/community-and-culture/melungeon-heritage/.

Batchelder, Ann, and the Delineator Home Institute. *New Delineator Recipes*. Butterick, 1929.

Bilheux, Roland, and Alain Escoffier. *The Professional French Pastry Series: Doughs, Batters, and Meringues*. Van Nostrand Reinhold Company, 1988.

Bir, Sara. "A Guide to Loaf Pans." Simply Recipes, May 22, 2024. https://www.simplyrecipes.com/the_simply_recipes_guide_to_loaf_pans/.

Blanner, Julie. "Loaf Pan Sizes." Julie Blanner, October 16, 2023. https://julieblanner.com/loaf-pan-sizes/.

Bousel, Joshua. "Chocolate Gravy Recipe." *Serious Eats*, April 26, 2019. https://www.seriouseats.com/chocolate-gravy-recipe.

Castle, Sheri. "Red-Eye Gravy." *Southern Living*, November 17, 2024. https://www.southernliving.com/recipes/red-eye-gravy.

"Columbia's Biscuit Queen." *Columbia Daily Tribune*, May 20, 2015. https://www.columbiatribune.com/story/news/2015/05/20/columbia-s-biscuit-queen/21761989007/.

"Country Ham and Red Eye Gravy Recipe." *What's Cooking America*, June 22, 2021. https://whatscookingamerica.net/history/countryhamhistory.htm.

Egerton, John. *Southern Food: At Home, on the Road, in History*. Knopf, 1987.

Finding AfroHistory. "Alexander Ashbourne: Pioneering the Biscuit Cutter Era." *Finding AfroHistory* (blog), April 26, 2024. https://findingafrohistory.com/alexander-p-ashbourne-black-inventor/.

Freeman, Debra. "The Rise: A History of American Biscuits." *King Arthur Baking*, January 30, 2023. https://www.kingarthurbaking.com/blog/2023/01/30/history-of-american-biscuits.

Hultquist, Mike. "Red Eye Gravy Recipe." *Chili Pepper Madness*, November 20, 2023. https://www.chilipeppermadness.com/recipes/red-eye-gravy/.

Jessee, Catherine, and Nicole Hopper. "Red-Eye Gravy." *Serious Eats*, June 5, 2024. https://www.seriouseats.com/red-eye-gravy-recipe-8640434.

Kelly, Leslie. "Why Southerners Are Obsessed With Chocolate Gravy (and Why You Should Be, Too)." *Allrecipes*, September 15, 2021. https://www.allrecipes.com/article/what-is-chocolate-gravy/.

Kentucky Historical Society. "Lively Willoughby's Canned Biscuits." *Kentucky Innovations,* 2021. https://apps.legislature.ky.gov/LegislativeMoments/Moments21RS/web/legmo_29.pdf.

Kraft, Chris. "The History of Country Ham." *Garden & Gun,* August 29, 2017. https://gardenandgun.com/articles/history-country-ham/.

Mahon, Susan Hall. "City Ham vs. Country Ham: What Is the Difference?" *Southern Living,* March 17, 2024. https://www.southernliving.com/city-ham-vs-country-ham-7371987.

Marks, Tasha. "The Tea-rific History of Victorian Afternoon Tea." Britishmuseum.org, August 14, 2020. https://www.britishmuseum.org/blog/tea-rific-history-victorian-afternoon-tea.

Martin, Mackenzie, and Suzanne Hogan. "Annie Fisher's Beaten Biscuit Empire," August 30, 2023. https://www.kcur.org/history/2023-08-30/annie-fishers-path-to-fame-paved-with-beaten-biscuits-from-missouri-was-nearly-forgotten.

McKie, Robin. "Do You Pronounce 'scone' to Rhyme With 'cone' or 'gone'? It Depends Where You're From." *The Guardian,* December 2, 2017. https://www.theguardian.com/science/2017/apr/23/how-do-you-pronounce-scone-answer-says-a-lot-english-language-day-shakespeare-birthday.

Miller, Chuck. "Faster Than a Speeding Biscuit?" Southeastern Railway Museum, May 21, 2022. https://www.train-museum.org/2022/05/21/faster-than-a-speeding-biscuit/.

Plesa, Aimee. "Do You Know the Muffin Man? A Brief History of Muffins in America." *Warren County Post,* September 8, 2020. https://warrencountypost.com/g/springboro-oh/n/16180/do-you-know-muffin-man-brief-history-muffins-america-publish-sept-8.

Reed, Jubilee P. "Beaten Biscuits." Living Heritage Museum, April 30, 2024. https://www.livingheritagemuseum.org/2024/04/30/12322/beaten-biscuits.

Rummel, Rachel. "Chocolate Gravy." *Atlas Obscura,* n.d. https://www.atlasobscura.com/foods/chocolate-gravy.

Rust, Randal. "Melungeons." Tennessee Encyclopedia, March 1, 2018. https://tennesseeencyclopedia.net/entries/melungeons/.

ShanOre Irish Jewelry. "Irish Scones History and Facts + Recipe." ShanOre Irish Jewlery, September 30, 2022. https://www.shanore.com/blog/irish-scones-history-and-facts-recipe/.

Smith, Andrew F. *The Oxford Encyclopedia of Food and Drink in America.* Oxford University Press, 2004.

St Pierre. "What Is Brioche? 10 Things You Need to Know About Brioche." *St Pierre UK* (blog), January 17, 2025. https://stpierrebakery.co.uk/blog/10-things-to-know-about-brioche/.

"The History of Country Ham and Red Eye Gravy." Food History, n.d. https://www.kitchenproject.com/history/RedEyeGravy/index.htm.

Thompson, Sharon. "Chocolate Gravy Has a Strong Southern Tradition." *State Journal-Register,* April 7, 2010. https://www.sj-r.com/story/lifestyle/food/2010/04/07/chocolate-gravy-has-strong-southern/41727084007/.

Traub, Courtney. "French Brioche: Short History of a Popular Sweet Bread." *Paris Unlocked,* July 19, 2023. https://www.parisunlocked.com/food/food-history/french-brioche-history-where-to-taste/.

INDEX

D

E

L

M

N

O

P

ABOUT THE AUTHOR

Paula L. Haney is the founder of Chicago's beloved Hoosier Mama Pie Company and author of the acclaimed *The Hoosier Mama Book of Pie*. With over two decades of experience in fine dining and pastry arts, Paula has redefined the art of pie-making, blending classic American traditions with innovative flavors. Her work has been featured in *Bon Appétit*, *Food & Wine*, and the Food Network. When not baking, she enjoys teaching and mentoring future pastry chefs. Paula lives in Chicago with her family, who continue to be her most enthusiastic taste-testers.